Wales and The Marches by Rail

A guide to the routes, scenery and towns

ABOUT THIS BOOK

Wales and the Marches by Rail is one of a series of guide-books compiled by the Railway Development Society, the independent voluntary body for rail-users.

We invite you to explore the Principality of Wales by InterCity train, diesel multiple unit, and behind vintage steam locomotives, in which the journey will be as pleasant an experience as the places you will visit.

Parts of the neighbouring English counties of Gloucestershire, Hereford and Worcester, Shropshire, and Cheshire are also included in this guide, since their history is often intertwined with that of Wales and their ancient towns and cities have long been gateways to the Principality.

Our guide-book covers all the British Rail lines in Wales and the Marches and the longer of the preserved lines. We have not described all the 'Great Little Trains of Wales' in detail, however, as many books have already been published about them. What we have tried to do is publicise some of the routes and places about which less has been written.

As Editor, I am grateful to all members of the Railway Development Society and local rail-users' groups who have written articles and supplied photographs for the book. Thanks are also due to Steven Binks for the line diagrams and to Neale Elder for the map; to John Lark and Trevor Garrod for editorial assistance; and to Simon Norton, Chris Magner, and the Ffestiniog Railway for some additional information.

We have written for the general reader, but the inclusion of some railway terms was unavoidable. The up line or platform is that used by trains travelling towards London; the down line being the opposite. DMU stands for diesel multiple unit, or railcar. InterCity 125 or High Speed Train is the powerful express train, with a diesel engine at either end, operating mainline services to South Wales. Narrow-gauge lines are those with less than the standard 4 feet 8½ inches between the rails – and Wales has several of these, mainly operated by preservation societies.

Every effort has been made to include up-to-date information; but we shall be pleased to receive any comments or updates for incorporation in any future edition.

Adrian Fawcett,
Editor.

CONTENTS

Llandudno.

CHESTER–LLANDUDNO
by Ray Brooks

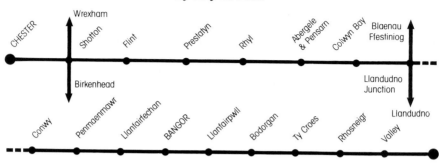

Chester is the gateway to North Wales. Known as 'Deva' to the Romans, it lies on the right bank of the River Dee, 7 miles above its estuary. In the Middle Ages, Chester owed its prosperity to its port, but when the river began to silt up, it lost its trade to Liverpool. It is possible to walk along the entire length of the walls, which are remarkably well preserved, and which, unlike those of any other ancient city in Britain, completely encircle the historic city centre. Chester has a beautiful Cathedral built, like the walls, of red sandstone. Unique to Chester are the famous 'Rows' – arcades forming continuous passages along the first floors of houses and shops. The city's many black and white half-timbered buildings give it a medieval air, though most are Victorian. Being the county town of Cheshire, it is an important commercial and administrative centre, with a population of 117,000.

Chester is also an important railway junction. No less than six different routes converge on it, including the 84½-mile Chester–Holyhead line, which was opened in 1850. Chester General Station itself is an attractive building – especially now that parts of it have been restored; as with other stations on the line, it was designed by the railway architect Francis Thompson.

Our route out of Chester takes us through tunnels, under the city walls, over the Shropshire Union Canal, and past the Roodee – the site of Chester Races since 1540. After crossing the Dee at Roodee Junction, we continue a short distance to Saltney Junction, where we part company with the former Great Western line to Wrexham and Shrewsbury. A bridge just past the junction marks our entry into Wales.

We are now in the county of Clwyd, heading north-west towards the coast. Our course is along flat reclaimed land; the canalised Dee lies out of sight on the right. The industrial suburbs of Chester extend for some 3½ miles to Mold Junction, the site of a derelict marshalling yard. Crosville buses run to Mold, the small pleasant county town of Clwyd, from Chester and Flint.

After Mold Junction, we pass on the left Hawarden Airport, which is used mainly by British Aerospace's Broughton works. Green fields as far as Queensferry are fast succumbing to the bulldozer, as the number of light industrial plants continues to grow. The line here is closer to the river, which it still parallels.

Shotton, our first stop, also serves Queensferry, which boasts a large sports complex, and Connah's Quay, whose eminence as a port has greatly declined and whose name derives from a local publican. At Shotton it is possible to connect with trains on the Wrexham–Birkenhead line, which crosses ours by an overbridge. On the right, across the Dee, is the steel rolling mill which was established in the 1890s by the firm of John Summers; its size and capacity has been considerably reduced in recent years as a result of British Steel Corporation's rationalisation plans.

4

We pass in turn on the right the former dock at Connah's Quay, where there is also a wagon works, and a disused coal-fired power-station which, rather surprisingly, provides a sanctuary for birds. We then emerge from Rockliffe Hall Tunnel and, as we reach the end of the canalised section of the Dee, the scenery changes: salt-marshes open up on the right, while to the left the Clwydian Hills come into view.

Flint, our next stop, is noted for its castle, which can just be seen from the station, behind some council houses on the right. Begun in 1277, the castle was the first of Edward I's Welsh fortresses. It was the scene of Edward II's meeting with Piers Gaveston in 1299 after the latter's return from exile; and of Richard II's imprisonment in 1399 at the hands of Bolingbroke (soon to be King Henry IV), which Shakespeare described in *Richard II*.

Leaving Flint, we can see on the left more light industrial development sandwiched between the hills and railway. To the right, low-lying farmland extends to the embankments of the ever-widening Dee, beyond which the towns of Neston, Heswall, and West Kirby on the Wirral Peninsula are visible on a clear day. We pass Bagillt on the left and, a little farther on, Courtauld's two former textile factories at Greenfield. Beyond the factories we pass Holywell Junction, formerly serving the short, steeply graded branch line to Holywell.

Holywell is a small town with 8,900 inhabitants. At St Winefride's Well here, tradition has it that Winefride, a local princess, was miraculously restored to life by St Beuno after having been beheaded by Caraduc, a prince from Hawarden. Buses run to Holywell from Flint.

After Holywell Junction, the landscape becomes more rural, with wooded hills on the left. Standing incongruously in dry dock at Llannerchymor is the *Duke of Lancaster*, a former Irish Sea car ferry. At Mostyn, which once possessed an ironworks, rail sidings still connect the docks; the principal rail freight is sulphur bound for the chemical works at Amlwch on the Isle of Anglesey.

From Mostyn to Point of Ayr the railway runs for 2 miles or so beside the estuary, where at low tide many wading birds can be seen on the mud-flats, and at high tide small coasters heading for Mostyn. Point of Ayr marks the mouth of the Dee. Most of the coal workings from the large colliery here extend beneath the sea; recent developments include a new drift-mine and a prototype coal-to-oil liquefaction plant.

After the disused station at Talacre, our route veers westward, passing the first of a long succession of caravan camps, as it follows the coastline.

Presently we reach the resort of Prestatyn, situated between the sea and the hills. It lies at the northern end of Offa's Dyke Path, which follows the ancient demarcation line built in about 800 by King Offa of Mercia. The trail officially begins at the summit of the hillside above the town – but many hikers like to wet their boots in the sea before embarking on the 168-mile trek to Chepstow in Gwent. It is waymarked throughout and surely ranks as one of Britain's great walks. A large new leisure centre on the sea-front, however, caters for holiday-makers who prefer less energetic pursuits.

Between Prestatyn and Rhyl the Vale of Clwyd opens out to the south, where the line is bordered by rough grazing land interspersed with housing. The sea to the north is obscured behind bungalow estates and caravan sites.

Rhyl is a lively modern resort, offering sandy beaches, safe bathing, a 2-mile-long promenade, a fun-fair and amusements. The Suncentre, in particular, has all the facilities popularly associated with a tropical resort, including a surfing-pool, a monorail, and palm trees.

For those wishing to venture farther afield, Crosville buses run along the Vale of Clwyd to Rhuddlan, St Asaph, Denbigh, and Ruthin. Rhuddlan is visited for its castle which, like so many others in the Principality, was the work of Edward I. It was here that in 1284 he issued his statute providing for the government of Wales. At St Asaph

Rhyl.

both cathedral and city are the smallest in Britain. Both Denbigh and Ruthin have castles, but that at Ruthin is privately owned and not normally open to the public.

Leaving Rhyl, the railway enters a stone-walled cutting. As we emerge from it, a view opens up on the right of the Marine Lake, with the fun-fair in the distance. Round the lake can be seen the track, and at the height of the season the train, of the 15-inch-gauge Rhyl Marine Lake Railway, built in the 1900s. Immediately past the lake, the line crosses the River Clwyd. To the right, at the river-mouth, is a distinctive steel-arched road bridge, beyond which lies Foryd Harbour. The trackbed of the former Vale of Clwyd line veers sharply to the left, but we continue on a straight course across the flat *morfa* – or land reclaimed from the Clwyd Estuary. New housing is encroaching on land not given over to caravans. From here, our route hugs the shoreline; a sea-wall protects it from incursions of the sea.

Abergele and Pensarn is our next stop. Abergele lies 1 mile inland; its busy cattle market is held on Mondays. This market town is joined to Pensarn, a modest seaside resort.

Resuming our journey beside the sea, we are joined by the A55, a road which parallels the railway for the next 20 miles or so. At the time of writing, vast sums are being spent on its realignment, and evidence of major roadworks can be seen

6

almost everywhere along it. We pass Gwrych Castle, a huge mock-medieval edifice built in 1815 and now used as a leisure centre.

At Llandulas, the railway crosses by an impressive bridge the diminutive Afon Llandulas before being crossed in its turn by the road, which then takes the seaward side. One benefit to rail passengers of the roadworks here is that they have removed the cutting on the seaward side, giving good views of two jetties used at high tide to load locally quarried stone on to coasters.

The new road skirts Penmaen Head, while the railway tunnels through it, emerging on an embankment above the promenade at Old Colwyn; the road then dives under the railway, which it parallels on the landward side. We run beside the promenade to Colwyn Bay Station, opposite which there is the stub of a pier — the only one surviving in Clwyd — providing the usual amusements and a discothèque. Colwyn's abundant sandy beach is safe for bathing. A notable attraction is the Welsh Mountain Zoo, situated in the south-west of the town, on a 37-acre estate overlooking the bay. The Safari Restaurant, with a balcony above the lion compound, is a feature of the zoo, which can be reached by minibus from the station.

From Colwyn Bay road and rail run side by side for several miles. As we journey west, the mountains of Snowdonia come into sight on the far side of the Conwy Valley.

Our entry into Gwynedd is heralded by yet more roadworks. Here work is well in hand on building a tunnel to take the A55 under the River Conwy — a project exceeded in cost and magnitude only by the Channel Tunnel. The decision to construct a tunnel was influenced by aesthetic factors: a bridge across the Conwy would have irreparably marred the famous view of the estuary and castle. Joining the mainline from the left is the scenic branch line to Blaenau Ffestiniog.

At Llandudno Junction passengers may make connections with local trains to Llandudno itself and Blaenau Ffestiniog, as well as to Holyhead. The line to Holyhead veers leftward to Conwy Castle, whereas that to Llandudno passes under the trunk road to follow the river estuary. As our train proceeds north, we may obtain a good view of Conwy town and castle across the river. Closer to hand, the mud-flats provide a haunt for wading birds and an anchorage for yachts.

But the tranquillity of the scene is broken by the noise of work on the road tunnel. The tunnel itself will be formed from a series of massive precast-concrete sections, for which the casting bays can be seen on the opposite side of the river at Conwy Morfa; each of these sections will then be sunk into a trench dredged in the bed of the estuary. The project is due for completion in 1990.

Deganwy is a small holiday resort and suburb of Llandudno from which it is separated by two golf-courses. The prominent headland of the Great Orme on the left heralds our arrival at Llandudno.

Llandudno lies on level ground between the Great Orme and the Little Orme. In 1850 it was little more than a village, and owes its development to the coming of the railway. Today, although offering all the facilities visitors would expect to find at a popular seaside resort, it retains something of its original Victorian dignity and elegance, and, unlike Rhyl, has eschewed some of the more vulgar forms of commercialism. The principal hotels line the promenade, which sweeps for 2 miles round the beach and the bay. Running parallel with it, two streets behind, is Mostyn Street, the main shopping centre. The station is conveniently situated to serve the full length of the bay, though the greater part of the town lies west of it, towards the Great Orme.

From the foot of the Great Orme, the 2,296-foot-long Victorian pier juts out to sea; it has a pier-head concert hall and a landing-stage for steamers, although there are no longer regular sailings. However, a new attraction on the slopes overlooking it is an all-weather artificial ski-track. The summit of the Great Orme at 679 feet can be ascended by the unique 3-foot-6-inch-gauge cable tramway, which runs from

Church Walks or — but not for the faint-hearted! — by the cabin lift, which, at 1 mile, is the longest passenger cable-car system in Britain, and which departs from Happy Valley. From the top can be seen, in the south-west, the peaks of Snowdonia, farther to the west, the Isle of Anglesey, and, to the north on an exceptionally clear day, the Isle of Man and mountains of Cumbria.

Wild goats, the descendants of a herd donated in 1900 by the Shah of Persia, graze on the slopes of the Great Orme. In winter they descend and can often be observed foraging for food in nearby gardens.

Associated with Llandudno was Charles Lutwidge Dodgson, better known as Lewis Carroll, the author of *Alice in Wonderland* and *Alice Through the Looking Glass*. Dodgson spent his holidays here, and the White Rabbit is said to have been inspired by one he saw along Llandudno's West Shore. A memorial portraying the White Rabbit was unveiled in 1933 by Lloyd George.

LLANDUDNO JUNCTION–HOLYHEAD
by Ray Brooks

After leaving Llandudno Junction, our train traverses The Cob, which was originally built by Thomas Telford and later widened to accommodate the railway. Ahead of us stand the three bridges spanning the River Conwy. The oldest of them — Telford's graceful suspension bridge — was opened in 1826; and until 1958, when it was replaced by a new road bridge, it carried the main London to Holyhead road. Robert Stephenson's tubular railway bridge, opened in 1848, served as a prototype for his larger Britannia Bridge across the Menai Strait. Each track is enclosed in a 410-foot-long wrought-iron tube. The imposing castellated portals at either end blend well with the castle.

Once over the river, our route takes us beneath the castle walls, through an arch in the town walls — the setting for innumerable pictures of the Irish Mail boat train — to Conwy's recently reopened station.

For a good view of the castle and bridges, take the path at the east end of the down platform, which leads to the mouth of the Afon Gyffin, a tributary of the Conwy, and proceed as far as the bowling-green. To reach the castle entrance, go under the railway bridge and through an arched gateway in the town walls to Castle Square.

Conwy Castle ranks among the most picturesque of Welsh fortresses, occupying a commanding position at the foot of the hills overlooking the river. It was begun in 1283 by Edward I and completed some four and a half years later.

Contemporary with the castle are the town walls. They extend for 1,400 yards round three sides of the town at an average height of 30 feet, and incorporate twenty-one towers and three gateways. Today it is still possible to walk along sections of them.

Other historic buildings open to the public are Plas Mawr, an attractive Elizabethan house; and Aberconwy House, a fifteenth-century merchant's dwelling.

The quay provides moorings for a variety of small fishing and pleasure craft, and a boarding-point for boat trips along the estuary. Facing the quay stands the smallest house in Britain — it has yet to be beaten by a converted broom cupboard in London!

Beyond the station, the railway tunnels under the walls, emerging in a cutting before crossing the present main road at Conwy Morfa. Formerly a Territorial Army camp and latterly a caravan site, Conwy Morfa has now become a vast building site for the road tunnel project described earlier. Journeying westwards again, we approach the sea, passing on the left Conwy Mountain and Penmaenbach Headland. The rail tunnel through the latter is paralleled by a new road tunnel. As we leave the tunnel behind, the hills recede and the sea appears once more on the right.

Conwy Castle. (*Photo:* Robert Barton)

As Penmaenmawr comes into view, the hills close in again. Penmaenmawr is a small resort, with a population of 4,000. Among its distinguished visitors in the past was William Gladstone. It is the starting-point for a variety of walks in the surrounding hills, including the ascent of the 1,550-foot-high Penmaenmawr, the headland from which the little town takes its name. Some of the granite quarried here is used by British Rail as ballast.

Between Penmaenmawr and Llanfairfechan the railway must negotiate the cliffs of Pen-y-clip, and is forced to tunnel. The present road is also a spectacular feat of engineering, with tunnels and a viaduct, of which the latter is best seen from the left side of the carriage.

The terrain changes as we draw near Llanfairfechan, a quiet seaside resort about the same size as Penmaenmawr. Like its neighbour, it too is a centre for several attractive walks, details of which may be obtained locally.

After Llanfairfechan the hills retreat slightly. Beyond the low-lying fields on the right is the Menai Strait, across which the outlines of Puffin Island and the much larger Isle of Anglesey may be discerned. Our journey continues through pleasant countryside. On the right stands Penrhyn Castle, the former seat of Lord Penrhyn. It is ostentatiously Victorian neo-Norman in style, with a keep modelled on that of Rochester Castle. Now owned by the National Trust, it contains a collection of dolls and an industrial railway museum. Some of the locomotives exhibited there were used on a narrow-gauge line linking Lord Penrhyn's quarry at Bethesda with his harbour at Port Penrhyn. We can glimpse the route of the old mineral line below the viaduct over which we travel before entering the 912-yard-long tunnel leading to Bangor Station.

The cathedral and university city of Bangor has a population of 16,750. It exudes a distinctly Cambrian atmosphere, with Welsh being widely spoken. Its mile-long pedestrianised High Street makes it a popular shopping centre for the surrounding district. It also boasts a Victorian pier, which has recently been restored.

Bangor Station was once an important junction, but now the only public transport links are by bus. Gwynedd's bus services are co-ordinated by the County Council under the collective title Bws Gwynedd. Timetables covering the area of each district council may be obtained from the County Planning Department or local information centres. Buses from Bangor start from the bus station near the Cathedral.

For the visitor the most useful services will be those to Caernarfon, Llanberis, and the Isle of Anglesey. Take the bus to Caernarfon to visit the magnificent thirteenth-century castle, the scene in 1969 of the investiture of HRH The Prince of Wales. From Caernarfon there is a more frequent service to Llanberis: there, visit the Slate Quarrying Museum, ride on the Padarn Lake Railway, and ascend the 3,560 feet of Snowdon – either on foot or by the mountain railway. Buses from Bangor to Anglesey serve the beautiful castle at Beaumaris, and interesting small towns such as Menai Bridge, Llangefni, and Amlwch. Others run to Porthmadog and Pwllheli, linking the Cambrian Coast Railway.

Immediately after its departure from Bangor our train enters Belmont Tunnel. Look right on leaving it for a glimpse of the town of Menai Bridge on the Isle of Anglesey and Telford's magnificent suspension bridge. Built in 1826, it has a span of 579 feet and towers 100 feet above high-water-level so as not to impede the passage of ships through the strait. Near here the wooden-walled training ship HMS *Conway* met its end on the rocks when under tow by a modern tug.

After passing the site of Menai Bridge Station and the former junction for Caernarfon, the line curves sharply to the right and is singled for the crossing of Britannia Bridge. From 1850 until 1970 – when it was unfortunately destroyed by fire – the bridge resembled that at Conwy, with each track enclosed in a wrought-iron tube; the only significant difference was its greater dimensions. When it was rebuilt, steel arches were attached to its original stone piers to support a new deck. An advantage of the reconstructed bridge is that rail travellers can now enjoy an uninterrupted view of the strait from both sides of the train. Overhead is a more recent addition, the new road deck carrying the A5 trunk road.

Once in Anglesey – Ynys Mon – we head towards the village whose fame stems from its name alone. Abbreviated for convenience on the timetable to Llanfairpwll, its full name is Llanfairpwllgwyngyllgogerychwyrndrobwllllantysiliogogogoch. Like many Welsh place-names, it is descriptive, and may be translated as 'St Mary's Church in the hollow by the white hazel close to the rapid whirlpool by the red cave of St Tysilio'.

Llanfairpwll occupies an important place in the annals of the Women's Institute; for the first branch in Britain was founded here in 1915.

Alight at the station – which has been developed as a tourist attraction in its own right by the knitwear company Pringle of Scotland – and climb the 115 steps to the

Telford's Menai Bridge.

top of the 100-foot-high Anglesey Column, built in 1817 to commemorate the first Marquess, a cavalry commander at the Battle of Waterloo, where he lost a leg.

As our train pulls away from Llanfairpwll, we may savour a restrospective view of the mountains of Snowdonia, particularly attractive on a clear winter's day when the tops are snow covered. Our route now runs through lush rolling countryside reminiscent of Ireland, with whitewashed cottages scattered here and there. Presently we pass Gaerwen, the junction for a freight-only line to the chemical plant at Amlwch, and cross on a long embankment the flat Malltraeth Marsh through which the little River Cefni flows south-westwards on its way to the sea.

We then pass in turn four unstaffed halts, whose survival owes much to their remoteness from the main road. Bodorgan, the first of them, is followed by Ty Croes whose name means 'House at the crossroads'. Rhosneigr is next, serving a small seaside resort, notorious in the eighteenth century for shipwreckers who hid in the Crigyll Estuary to the north. Immediately following on the left are the runways of

RAF Valley, a training airfield opened in 1941 and noted for its flight of helicopters whose air—sea rescue missions have recovered many casualties from the sea and mountains; the annual open day in September attracts thousands of visitors. Beyond the airfield lies the village of Valley, the last of the halts. Our approach is marked on the right by sidings serving Wylfa nuclear power-station. Here, British Rail's policy of bilingual station naming may cause confusion: the name Dyffryn — Welsh for 'valley' — appears on the nameboard, whereas Y Fali — a more colloquial term — is used on road signs.

On the last lap of our journey, we are joined once more by the A5 and, in its company, cross the 1,200-yard-long Stanley Embankment which connects Holy Island with the Isle of Anglesey, through which the tide races on the ebb and flow. Holy Island, on which the town of Holyhead with its important harbour is situated, measures only 7½ miles at its longest and 3½ miles at its widest point. At the west end of the embankment the road leaves the railway, and we pass in succession on the right Penrhos Nature Reserve, the Anglesey Aluminium Company (who, incidentally, also own the nature reserve), and Holyhead locomotive depot. On the left stands Holyhead Mountain, or Mynydd Twr, from the 710-foot-high summit of which Snowdon can be seen.

We finally arrive at Holyhead Station, the end of our 84½-mile journey from Chester. The station is situated at the base of the Inner Harbour; its four platforms are arranged in the form of the letter V, with Platform 1 forming the left arm, and Platforms 2, 3, and 4 the right. Farther to the right lies the Freightliner terminal where containers are transferred between ship and train. Although the track layout remains unchanged, the station now lacks the presence given by the former hotel, the demolition of which removed a prominent landmark.

Sealink's regular ferry on the route between Holyhead and Dun Laoghaire (pronounced 'Dun Lairey') is the 7,836-ton purpose-built St Columba. When in port, she ties up at the quay alongside Platform 1, where the Customs and Emigration offices are located. One word of warning: because of the station's geography, ferry passengers wishing to board a train may face a long walk if it departs from Platforms 2, 3, or 4. Sealink's twice-daily sailings to Dun Laoghaire are complemented by B & I's to Dublin. However, the latter are less convenient for rail passengers, since they berth some distance away from the station at Admiralty Pier.

For a panoramic view of the railway and harbour, turn left and left again after leaving the station, follow the railway wall, then ascend a path to a granite obelisk. This is also a good vantage point from which to observe the ferry's arrival.

To reach the main shopping area, turn right into Victoria Road from the station; after the bus garage, turn left and proceed along Market Street and Stanley Street.

For a closer look at the port, continue along Victoria Road to Marine Square, where the Tourist Information Centre is situated. To the right lies Salt Island and Admiralty Pier, at the entrance to which stands a Doric arch built in 1821 to commemorate a visit by George IV, and to mark the end of the A5. Turn right at the base of the pier to see the New Harbour. Opened in 1873, it is protected by a breakwater that extends 7,869 feet out to sea — the longest in Britain. A broad-gauge railway was used for its construction and maintenance until 1913.

Holyhead, with a population of 10,500, is known to Welsh-speakers as Caer Gybi, which means the 'Fortress of St Cybi'. But despite its Welsh name, it has a cosmopolitan air typical of many ferry ports, with a melange of Welsh, Irish, and Merseyside accents. Like Fishguard, it is in many ways the Land's End of Wales: the way forward lies over the sea. But it must not be forgotten that the return trip may be as enjoyable as the outward one, offering a fresh perspective of the farming, mountains, estuaries, bridges, castles, seaside resorts, and industries of North Wales. Diolch yn fawr, croeso'r yn ôl.

LLANDUDNO JUNCTION–BLAENAU FFESTINIOG–THE CONWY VALLEY LINE

by David Sallery

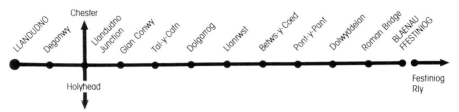

The 28 miles of single-track railway linking the mainline at Llandudno Junction and Blaenau Ffestiniog offer some of the most picturesque and spectacular scenery anywhere in Britain.

Our train, which has probably come from Llandudno, leaves the mainline just outside the station. There is soon evidence of the earthworks involved in the construction of the Conwy bypass. An area of marshland, formerly rich in wildlife, has been enclosed and drained as part of this scheme. Having passed this 'enclosure', we are presented with a very fine view of the Conwy Estuary at its widest point. Conwy Castle, with its attendant bridges and town walls, is clearly seen as is the embankment carrying the main road and railway. We soon arrive at our first stop – Glan Conwy. Like all the stations from now on, this is unstaffed, tickets being taken and issued by the conductor-guard. Another point of interest is the set of wooden steps to assist passengers in and out of the train. This station, and also the one at Dolgarrog, have been reopened in recent years, having formerly been closed under the Beeching Plan. At low tide, the marshes here, and indeed the whole length of the tidal River Conwy, are a paradise for bird-watchers – herons, curlews, oyster-catchers, to name but a few, are clearly visible.

Leaving Glan Conwy behind, the estuary now begins to narrow. We continue south, following the river's every turn, with the hills and mountains becoming noticeably closer. Hidden among the trees to our left are the celebrated Bodnant Gardens, owned by the National Trust, and well worth a visit.

Our next stopping-point is Tal-y-Cafn. The road bridge over the Conwy here replaced a ferry crossing, which had existed since Roman times. One of the local highlights is the annual raft race, which takes place between this point and Conwy. Many strange craft can be seen navigating the course at this time. Shortly after leaving Tal-y-Cafn, the ancient church of Caerhun is seen, surrounded by yew trees, on the opposite bank. Near by are the remains of the Roman settlement of Canovium. If you follow the lines of pylons to the skyline, you will see the historic pass of Bwlch Ddeufaen. This was the route of the Roman road from Canovium to Segontium (Caernarfon). It was also a stage-coach route from Anglesey and Ireland, before the coastal route via Penmaenmawr was built. Continuing in close proximity to the river, the nearest conical peak, on our right, is Pen-y-Gaer, site of a well-preserved Iron Age hill-fort. Our next calling-point is Dolgarrog. This village leapt to prominence in 1925, when a dam supplying hydroelectric power built above the village, gave way. The ensuing flood caused sixteen deaths, and many injuries. The gash in the old dam walls is still visible high up in the hills as a sombre reminder. The bridge over the river here originally carried a siding to the aluminium works, visible on the right. This provides the main source of employment for Dolgarrog. The bridge is now, however, only safe for pedestrians. We continue up the slowly narrowing valley along a section very liable to flood in winter, the boulders along the side of the line being placed there in order to prevent the track being swept away as has happened quite frequently in the past.

We are now at the limit of the tidal Conwy, and the long straggling village across the river is Trefriw. This village is well known for its woollen-mills, and its chalybeate mineral-water springs, reputedly of medicinal value.

Our arrival at Llanrwst is marked by the crossing loop which comes just before the rather imposing station. This is the only passing loop on the branch line and, in the summer months, there is frequently another train awaiting our arrival. The interested observer may watch the exchange of metal tokens between our driver and the signalman. This process ensures complete safety in the working of trains on a single-track railway. Llanrwst is a pleasant little Welsh market town, and has a splendid bridge over the Conwy, built by Inigo Jones in 1636, and still in use today. Near by is Gwydr Castle, famed for its peacocks, and also the Welsh Museum of Wildlife.

Leaving Llanrwst, the heavily forested hill to our right was once a major centre for lead-mining. However, since those days, much reclamation has taken place, and there are some delightful signposted walks to be enjoyed. We now cross the River Conwy on a steel girder bridge, and enter the Snowdonia National Park. Very shortly we arrive in Betws-y-Coed. Although only a small village, it stands at the meeting-point of three rivers: the Lledr, which we will follow for the next part of our journey, the Llugwy, which flows down from Capel Curig and drains a large part of the Snowdon Massif, and, of course, the Conwy. Betws-y-Coed itself has much to interest the casual visitor, and it is a major centre for the tourist industry. At the station itself, a particular attraction is the Conwy Valley Railway Museum, and miniature trains may frequently be seen running alongside their larger counterparts. At the Stablau Visitor Centre can be found details of guided walks starting from stations along the line. Betws is also a starting-point for the Snowdon Sherpa bus service for spectacular trips round Snowdonia.

The next part of our journey is what really makes this railway line something special. Thus far, our journey has been along a pleasant pastoral river valley. However, we are about to enter the very heart of the Welsh Mountains. Although the line to Llanrwst was opened in 1863, and to Betws-y-Coed in 1868, a further eleven years elapsed before the first train steamed triumphantly into Blaenau Ffestiniog, on 22 July 1879. Indeed, at one time the London & North Western Railway seriously considered building the line to the narrow gauge of 1 foot 11½ inches, the same as the Ffestiniog Railway, because of the difficult terrain. Victorian fortitude prevailed, however, and one can readily appreciate from the train how steep and sinuous is the course eventually chosen.

Leaving the station, look out for the bridge on our left. This carries the main A5 London–Holyhead road, and the arch of the bridge has the inscription that it was built in the same year in which the Battle of Waterloo was fought — that is 1815.

Following a short spell in dense conifer forest, Beaver Pool Tunnel is followed by the stretch of water of that name. This can be glimpsed through the trees down to our left. This marks the confluence of the rivers Conwy and Lledr, our course following the latter. The upper stretch of the Conwy from this point is known as the 'Fairy Glen', and is a spectacular stretch of rocky pools and surging cataracts.

The harsher engine noise of our train gives a hint of the severe gradients which we now encounter as we continue up the narrow, thickly wooded valley. A temporary respite for the firemen of steam trains was provided by Gethins Bridge. This is a handsome, stone-built viaduct of seven arches, carrying us across the river and the main road. The track across the viaduct is level, and the difference from the steep gradients on either side is clearly visible through the front window of the train. Waterfalls and rock pools abound in the river, now well below us, and we enter the short, unlined rock tunnel emerging at Pont-y-Pant. Despite the apparent lack of houses, a large Youth Hostel near by contributes considerably to the passenger revenue. A spectacular waterfall on the River Lledr near by – well worth a visit – brings railway and river together again. A more gentle stretch of track follows past the water-meadows, and through another short tunnel to Dolwyddelan. The impressive peak rearing majestically to our right is Moel Siabod, at 2861 feet. Disused slate quarries are observed on both sides, this being the northern limit of the slate measures. Dolwyddelan is a picturesque village, and excellent rock-climbing is available in the vicinity. The old narrow-gauge diesel locomotive on the platform here is a foretaste of the attractions to be found at Gloddfa Ganol Slate and Railway Museum at Blaenau.

Leaving this station, to the right is the stark, square tower which is all that remains of the once-proud Dolwyddelan Castle. This was built by the native Welsh Prince Iorwerth in the twelfth century, and was the birthplace of Prince Llewelyn the Great, his son. The castle is steeped in Welsh mythology, and is open for visiting under the National Trust. Continuing up the valley, and through the short Bertheos Tunnel, Snowdon and its attendant peaks may be seen above the open moorland ahead. We have now parted company with the main road, which climbs steeply up to the Crimea Pass, much subject to blockage by snow in winter.

The charmingly named, and situated, Roman Bridge is followed by a further short tunnel. We continue up the narrow rocky valley, the wheel flanges of our train squealing on the incessant curvature as the train tries to seek out the most level path for our progress. A lonely stretch, with nothing but sheep for company, leads us to the north portal of the celebrated Ffestiniog Tunnel. This at 3,726 yards is the longest single-track tunnel, and the eighth longest tunnel over all, in Britain. Apart from a short curve at the north end, the tunnel is perfectly straight. Construction of this tunnel took four years of hard toil, amid flooding, rock-falls, and explosions.

British Rail and Ffestiniog Railway trains side by side at Blaenau Ffestiniog. (*Photo:* Tom Heavyside)

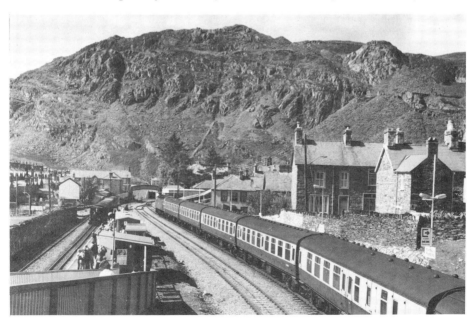

The extremely hard rock required special drills and consequently the tunnel needs no lining. The summit-level of the line at 790 feet, is in the middle of the tunnel, and after what always seems an age in the darkness, we suddenly burst into the open to be confronted by an astonishing vista. Few towns in Britain can have so spectacular an entrance as this, with vast heaps of slate waste towering precariously above and around us, and all in the shadow of lofty mountain peaks. The mounds to the right form part of what were formerly the Oakley slate quarries, nowadays the home of Gloddfa Ganol Slate Museum. This was once the largest slate-mine in the world, and had twenty-six floors, over a vertical difference of 1,400 feet with 50 miles of underground railways. The quarries to our left formed part of the Llechwedd complex, now home to the world-famous Miners' Tramway. Shortly afterwards, as the valley widens, the Ffestiniog Railway from Porthmadog parallels us for the short distance to Blaenau Ffestiniog Central Station. This station was newly opened in 1982, following the reopening throughout of the Ffestiniog Railway. We have now reached the limit for passenger trains on this route, although the line continues for a further 5 miles, to Trawsfynydd nuclear power station, from which there is a regular traffic in nuclear waste to Sellafield. Originally this line continued as far as Bala, where connection was made with the now-also-closed Ruabon–Barmouth line.

The delights of Blaenau Ffestiniog are many in number. The slate-mines, walking, rock-climbing, and views are unsurpassed – and the little-changed streets of the town itself give ample cause to remember a time when it was the slate capital of the world.

Train services on the Conwy Valley line are at their most frequent in the summer months, with eight trains each way on weekdays. In the winter months, a basic service of five trains each way is provided. Sunday services on the line are restricted to the peak months of July and August, when three trains daily are run. In previous years, the Sunday services were operated by Gwynedd County Council, who hired a train from BR. However BR now run the Sunday service. One aspect of the Sunday service worthy of mention is that members of the North Wales Railway Circle will be providing a running commentary of the journey, and also a service of light refreshments. Good connections are provided at Blaenau Ffestiniog for the magnificent journey to Porthmadog, on the Ffestiniog Railway. There are also connections available at Blaenau Ffestiniog to Gloddfa Ganol Slate and Railway Museum, and to Llechwedd Slate Caverns and Miners' Tramway. Both attractions are very highly recommended. A wide selection of special fare offers are available. These cover, among others, through journeys to the Ffestiniog Railway, Day Ranger and Evening Ranger tickets, and the Ffestiniog Link Circular Day Tour. Full details of the train services and fare offers are contained in the attractive leaflet published by BR, and available at manned stations and tourist centres.

FFESTINIOG RAILWAY
by Adrian Fawcett

Unlike many steam railways, the Ffestiniog Railway is not a working museum. It does, however, abound in industrial archaeology, and some of its locomotives and coaches go back over a hundred years. The line was opened in 1836 to carry slate from the quarries and mines at Blaenau Ffestiniog to the sea at Porthmadog for shipment to other parts of Britain and abroad. The loaded wagons ran down from Blaenau by gravity, and the empties were pulled back again by horses. The railway was laid to the narrow gauge of 1 foot 11½ inches, commonly known as '2 foot' because of the mountainous terrain necessitating sharp curves. Traffic outgrew the capacity of gravity and horses, and steam locomotives were introduced in 1863. Of the four original small engines, two survive, though in much-rebuilt form – *Princess* is in the Porthmadog Museum, while *Prince* belongs to the working stud of locomotives. The Ffestiniog was the first narrow-gauge railway to obtain permission to carry passengers – this service was inaugurated in 1865. In 1872, a further development was to take place which had great significance for rail travel. The metal-framed bogie coach, now almost universally used throughout the world, made its British, and possibly, its world début on the Ffestiniog. The two originals, numbered 15 and 16, are still in daily use during the summer service.

The last decades of the nineteenth century were the heyday of the Ffestiniog, when railway engineers came from all over the world to see what could be done on the narrow gauge, but after 1900 traffic and business declined. Several factors were responsible – the general decline in the slate industry, the arrival of standard-gauge railways to Blaenau, the decline of sea transport for purely coastal freight, and the decline of sailing-ships. Local passenger traffic also declined and, in 1939, passenger services ceased upon the outbreak of the Second World War. Slate trains ran about three times a week, but these, too, finished in 1946, and by this time the railway was in a very run-down state. Various people endeavoured to find a way to reopen the railway, but to no avail, until in the early 1950s a group of interested persons got together with Mr Alan Pegler, who offered to buy up the controlling shares in the company and to operate the railway with the assistance of a voluntary society.

From 1955 the line was reopened in stages and, by 1958, services were operating between Porthmadog and Tan-y-Bwlch – just over half the original route. This had been done on a shoestring, and there followed no less then ten years before any more of the line was reopened. This progressed in stages through to 1982 when the final section from Tanygrisiau into the town centre of Blaenau Ffestiniog was opened again. Today, the Ffestiniog Railway station adjoins the British Rail station, allowing an easy interchange.

The journey to Porthmadog takes sixty-five minutes. Alternatively, a round trip may be completed in two and a half hours. From Blaenau Ffestiniog, the railway briefly runs parallel to the BR lines, then curves away round the edge of the town, across a modern level crossing, followed by the small Bowydd River, before the first station is reached, at Tanygrisiau. From here, another modern level crossing is passed before the line skirts the banks of the Llyn Ystradau. This artificial lake is part of a pumped-storage hydroelectric power station, built by the British Electric Authority (now the CEGB) to even out the demand for electricity. Water is pumped up into the lake while demand is low, then is allowed to run back through turbines to generate power when necessary. The building of the power station involved the compulsory purchase of part of the route of the railway, and it took a long series of court cases to obtain compensation. It was not until 1971, sixteen years after the power station scheme was announced that the way was finally clear to restore trains to Blaenau.

The diversionary route now takes us through a tunnel, under a spur of the Moelwyn Mountains. After the tunnel, the original course of the railway can still be clearly seen to the left. We now descend by a complete spiral to Ddualt Station, where there is a picnic site and viewing table.

The next section of the line takes a tortuous course along the contours of a steep wooded valley. Tan-y-Bwlch Station comes next, with its island platform, in a picturesque setting. Shortly afterwards comes the first of two horseshoe bends as we curve through over 180 degrees to the left. At Plas Halt, which is close to the Snowdonia National Park Centre, we negotiate the second bend and we once again head towards Porthmadog. The railway now begins to lose height quite rapidly; between Blaenau and Porthmadog the line descends some 700 feet.

After the next station, at Penrhyn, the train enters more open countryside before reaching Minffordd Station. Here there is a rail interchange with the Cambrian Coast line. We cross over the BR route immediately beyond the station. After Boston Lodge

Porthmadog–Blaenau Ffestiniog train hauled by *Mountaineer* passes over The Cob. *(Photo:* Tom Heavyside)

Station, the line runs along The Cob, an embankment separating the estuary of the River Glaslyn from Cardigan Bay. Farther away to the right are the mountains of Snowdonia. Users of the parallel road across The Cob must pay a toll. Porthmadog Station is by the harbour in this pleasant little town. The BR station is much less central, a good ten minutes' walk away.

I am indebted to the Ffestiniog Railway's History leaflet, used in the preparation of this article.

Historical Note
Strictly speaking, the railway is the Festiniog Railway, spelt with one 'f'. The name was misspelt in the Act of Parliament authorising its construction, and to this day it has not been officially changed.

SHREWSBURY–CHESTER LINE
by David Lloyd

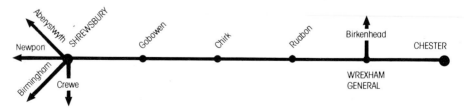

The traveller embarking on a rail journey between Shrewsbury and Chester can look forward to visions of many aspects of life in Britain. Few journeys can offer such a variety of landscape, either natural or man-made in origin. Hills, valleys, and plains all form part of the terrain across which this line passes. Glimpses of farmsteads standing proudly in fields of verdant green contrast vividly with the starkness of dereliction in former mining areas.

Commencing the journey amid the splendour of Shrewsbury's renovated station the traveller will no doubt have been impressed by the carnation buttonholes sported by railway staff. During the summer season this floral display is enhanced by many colourful hanging flower-baskets.

Pulling away from the Shrewsbury platform the line to Crewe can be seen immediately to the right of the train. An impressive lower-quadrant semaphore signal gantry guards the entrance to the north of Shrewsbury Station, controlled by the aptly named Crewe junction box which overlooks the parting of the routes.

An impression of the gradients followed by the Chester line is quickly evident as the train leaves Shrewsbury. After passing the cluster of tracks which form the remaining part of Coton Hill goods yard the train's engine begins to labour with the climb northwards up Coton Hill Bank. As the line levels out and the train accelerates, the site of Leaton Station is passed. Several small buildings still remain, but the signal-box finally closed in November 1987 when the manually operated gates on the level crossing were replaced by automatic half-barriers.

Woodland and pasture extend on either side of the track, evidence of the agricultural and forestry work on the North Shropshire Plain. The products of dairying and beef- and sheep-fattening find their way into the weekly markets of Shrewsbury and Oswestry.

When British Railways decided in 1960 to speed up the local passenger services between Shrewsbury and Chester eight stations and halts were closed. Considerable opposition was aroused in the case of Baschurch, Whittington, and Weston Rhyn. The efforts to retain the three villages' stations were in vain, and for over twenty years the only intermediate stations between Shewsbury and Chester have been Gobowen, Chirk, Ruabon, and Wrexham. Many former station buildings remain, however, among them Baschurch, but this one no longer boasts the peculiar wooden water-tower above the main structure, for this was removed by the Great Western Railway over half a century ago.

North of Baschurch is the site of Stanwardine Halt, once serving rural homesteads and the inhabitants of the hamlet of Weston Lullingfields. As the gradient descends, a bridge takes us over the River Perry, a tributary of the Severn. Drainage of land around the river has lowered levels to the extent that the foundations of this bridge were weakened. For this reason a speed limit has been applied to trains passing over it.

The railway enthusiast will be glad to see the appearance of the semaphore signals which proclaim the approach to Haughton sidings. Very much a GWR installation, it includes a goods refuge loop in the up direction. A down refuge siding was removed many years ago. How bleak it must have been in winter for the signalmen who worked this isolated box! Access was along narrow country lanes, and there is still no water or electricity in 1988. At that time the block instruments were still Spagnoletti singles, and only two upper-quadrant signals, the down starter and the up distant, had dared to trespass upon this rural GWR museum piece.

The line sweeps first to the west, then back to the north. Some evidence of the former Rednal Aerodrome may be seen to the right of the train. Its station, correctly known as Rednal and West Felton, follows shortly afterwards, and a clear view is given of the Montgomeryshire extension of the Shropshire Union Canal. How grand to have an Act of Parliament for the opening of a canal, for in 1987 legislation was passed to enable sections of this routeway to be reinstated for navigation.

As the train speeds along, the skyline is broken by the silhouettes of several oil storage tanks. This is the Whittington BP depot and accommodates road delivery vehicles which serve garages throughout North and Mid Wales. Improvements to the road network now allow the operation of large road tankers direct from the refineries such as Stanlow on the River Mersey, although the depot is still served by two or three block trains each week.

Immediately past the oil depot is an overbridge which once carried the A5 London–Holyhead trunk road. In December 1986 a bypass was completed and A5 traffic now crosses the railway north of Gobowen. The building of the new road meant that a once-busy road service station adjacent to the bridge lost so much traffic that it closed within months.

The village of Whittington was once a railway crossroads, for here the route eventually followed by the Oswestry, Ellesmere & Whitchurch Railway crossed the Shrewsbury–Chester line on an overbridge. Had plans come to fruition there would have been no less than three triangles linking the four routes, thus making it possible for Chester-bound trains to turn west to Oswestry or east to Ellesmere, and for trains from Ellesmere to travel northwards to Chester. It never happened, but Whittington did have two stations – High Level and Low Level. Both closed in 1960, though the Ellesmere–Oswestry line itself did not succumb until 1966.

A village such as Whittington hardly seems the place to encounter a vigorous campaign for the reopening of a station. During the 1980s pupils from Moreton Hall School, two villages away, embarked on an educational research project and discovered that Whittington had no direct bus service to Gobowen, the nearest station. Furthermore no buses served the village after 6 p.m., and there were none at all on Sundays. Many villages once served by railways have suffered this fate, but have times changed, and is there now a growing demand for access to trains?

Two miles to the north the train eventually stops to serve Gobowen. A shadow of its former self, almost every siding has been lifted, and only one signal-box remains. A branch line to Oswestry and Blodwell Quarry can be seen to the west, allowing a daily ballast train to gather a cargo. A coal concentration depot flourishes in the former goods yard. The station buildings, however, form a sad appearance. An elaborate plan to restore them to the 1848 condition was abandoned half-way through the programme.

North of Gobowen a modern concrete overbridge allows the A5 trunk road to cross the line at a new location. Most of the Shrewsbury–Chester Railway south of Ruabon was built under the Shrewsbury, Oswestry & Chester Junction Railway Act of 1845. The route to be taken as ordained in the Act would have brought the railway along a course followed by the new A5 to the right of the train. Dissent was registered to this proposal by Mary Deakin, guardian of the infant Elizabeth Deakin, who requested that the railway be built behind the mansion called Moreton Hall. Her wish was granted, and an Act of Deviation was passed in 1846 permitting line to be built on its present course. Moreton Hall is recognisable by the triangular-shaped building and one of the school's boarding-houses, to the right of our train as it enters Weston Rhyn.

Two small hills, one on either side of the track, encountered shortly before passing over the Weston Rhyn level crossing, are the sole remaining evidence of two small coal-mines which closed in 1871. These are claimed to be the farthest south of all the North Wales coalfield mines. Although there were several small mines in the vicinity of Weston Rhyn, a much larger one 3 miles to the east of Ifton operated until 1968, and was served by a branch line.

A strange happening took place at Weston Rhyn in 1965 when the Royal Train was brought to a stand in the dead of night by signals on its journey north. Such an almost unprecedented occurrence was brought to an end when eventually the signals were cleared. The story goes that the signalman in the Wrexham signal-box had dozed off, and was only aroused by the traffic inspector who was awaiting the train's arrival at Rossett box. His action by jumping into his car and racing to Wrexham to arouse the slumbering bobby allowed the train's passage northwards from Weston Rhyn. Rumour has it that the Queen Mother was on board. Did she ever discover her unscheduled visit to Weston Rhyn?

On a northward journey the rail traveller will see evidence of industrial activity on the landscape. Shortly before Chirk Station the Llangollen branch of the Ellesmere Canal can be seen to the right, crossing the Ceiriog Valley on a stone-built aqueduct. This was essentially a feeder to bring water from the River Dee above Llangollen to the Shropshire Union Canal system. The Glyn Valley Tramway has long closed, but evidence of it can be seen in an arch in the road bridge on its western side as the train stops at Chirk.

As the train leaves Chirk industrial scenes appear to the right, with Cadbury's and Kronospan dominating the scene. Both are served by private sidings, a new installation for the latter being put in during the early months of 1988.

Shortly before Chirk the canal tunnelled beneath the railway, so it now appears to the left of the train. The site of Whitehurst Halt is passed shortly before the A5 overbridge. Crossing the viaduct over the Dee Valley the rail traveller has no idea of the magnificence of this stone-built structure, but instead can look left out towards the beautiful Vale of Llangollen. Glimpses of one of Thomas Telford's most ambitious projects – the Pontcysyllte Aqueduct which carries the Llangollen Canal on stone piers linked by cast-iron troughs – may be seen in the Vale.

Once over the viaduct and past the site of Rhosymedre Halt the cutting through which trains vanished towards Llangollen, Corwen, Bala, Dolgellau, and Barmouth may be seen on the left. Ruabon was a busy junction. Today it is difficult to imagine that sixty-five men were employed on the railway here at one time.

North of Ruabon and passing the site of the station serving Johnston and Hafod there looms on the horizon clear evidence of coal-mining. Bersham Colliery finally closed in the latter months of 1986, and its signal-box in February 1987, the sidings being lifted afterwards. A mile farther on more sidings on either side of the train herald the approach to Wrexham, a town which in post-war years has seen many of its traditional industries decimated. It has fought back with great success, attracting many modern factories, but sadly few provide the substantial freight traffic of which the town could once boast. Only Croes Newydd North Fork signal-box remains of nearly twelve which controlled the passage of trains in and around Wrexham. There still remains access to the Brymbo branch which also serves the former Gatewen Colliery, but no traffic uses these rails. Wrexham General is the largest intermediate station on the Shrewsbury–Chester line. Platform 4 comprises the remains of the former London & North Eastern Railway Exchange Station, but can only be accessed by a long walk across a nearby road bridge. Why the footbridge linking General's platforms has not been extended to make public access to Exchange far simpler is a mystery.

Departing from Wrexham the Chester-bound traveller can witness the tracks of the Shotton–Bidston route on the left. The train enters the single-line section to Saltney Junction, controlled by the power signal-box in Chester. Clearly there is a downhill gradient, the Gresford Bank, a formidable obstacle to southbound heavy freight trains in the days of steam. Even today some trains proceeding to Wrexham find the climb hard going, and the falling leaves of autumn can play havoc with the slick operation needed to ensure that single-line working does not delay traffic. Much of the dereliction of mining activity has disappeared in landscape restoration projects, but the speed restriction on the northward descent of Gresford Bank is a reminder of possible mining subsidence. Years previously a disaster at Gresford Colliery caused the loss of many lives.

Gresford Halt can be identified by the station building, now a private residence, on the right. At the foot of the hill Rossett is passed. The singling of the line early in 1987 saw the final removal of the loops and sidings so often used to accommodate the Royal Train when stabled in the area.

As the train speeds across the Cheshire Plain agriculture once again dominates the scene, as this is good dairying territory. The North Wales route from Holyhead appears on the left and is joined by the Shrewsbury route at Saltney Junction. From here to Chester there were once four tracks, and in steam days it was common to see GWR and London Midland & Scottish Railway trains running parallel into Chester Station. The journey ends by crossing the Roodee bridges over the River Dee, and entry to Chester is made through short tunnels cut through the sandstone.

WREXHAM–BIDSTON

by Roderick Fairley

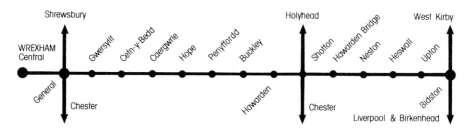

Wrexham, at the southern end of our line, is a pleasant town and a handy touring centre. Near by lies the Bersham Industrial Heritage Museum on the site of the former Bersham Colliery and the National Trust's Erddig Hall, and not far away is Llangollen Steam Railway.

Wrexham is surprising for a town of its size in that it still has two railway stations. Our journey on the 'friendly line', as it is known, starts at Wrexham Central, which is located only 200 yards from the High Street and the main shops. The station is but a shadow of its former self. It used to have three platforms – two to serve trains on the Cambrian line to Ellesmere and Oswestry, and a bay to serve trains from the Bidston line. All that is now left is the one platform that was the up line to Ellesmere where the trains now terminate, and one of those delightful concrete bus shelters. However, the shelter has been brightened up by having the montage of a DMU painted on the town side, and the station is popular with shoppers owing to its proximity to the town centre.

Our train leaves the platform and proceeds along the single track, with a speed limit of 15 m.p.h. On the right is the Wrexham Lager Brewery, makers of the excellent Wrexham Lager. The line now takes a sharp right-hand curve and passes under the Chester–Shrewsbury line, and ½ mile from Central we arrive at Wrexham General Platform 4. This platform and the disused one on the left used to be Wrexham Exchange, which was the original terminus of the Wrexham, Mold & Connah's Quay Railway. Over on the right can be seen the other three platforms of Wrexham General. To gain access you must cross the Chester–Shrewsbury line via the road bridge.

After a short stop we move off until our train reaches the signal-box where our driver gives up the token for the single-line section; we now accelerate and bear off to the left.

Some 1¾ miles after leaving Wrexham we arrive at Gwersyllt, a small village that has become more of a suburb of Wrexham. On the approaches to Gwersyllt, if you look out of the right-hand window, you will see the remains of the Great Western line that long ago used to climb to the mining areas in the hills above Wrexham. The line was so steep in places that inclines were used to ascend the steeper gradients. Our train moves off again and as we travel, to the right you can see across the Alyn and Dee valleys; on a clear day you can see over the Cheshire Plain.

The line now curves gently to the right, and if you look down you can see the edges of a very fine viaduct, one of the architectural gems of the line. We arrive at Cefn-y-Bedd which lies 4¼ miles from Central, and then on to Caergwrle. This village was a spa many years ago. Remains of the wells and mineral-water bottling plant can still be found in the woods to the east of the station. Special trains brought people from all over the North-West for the cure. There are also the remains of a castle that are worth a visit.

We now settle down for the journey of 5½ miles to Hope Station. On the left is Hope Mountain from the top of which the energetic can see spectacular views. On to Penyffordd where a branch line curves off to the left. This serves the Castle cement works – coal in and cement trains out. This branch originally joined the Chester–Denbigh line that until recently still continued for several miles to Mold. Passenger services ceased in the 1960s, but the line provided a freight service to a chemical works there. As we progress we pass over the trackbed of the Chester–Denbigh Railway and on the far side of the bridge can be seen the remains of Hope Exchange that provided transfer between the two railways. There was no road access to the station. The line climbs the 8 miles to Buckley, originally called Buckley Junction. As we approach the station, on the left can be made out the embankment that carried the Wrexham, Mold & Connah's Quay Railway up to Buckley. In the space of the 8 miles from Wrexham Central we have called at seven stations. Most of these stations have either been close to the village centre or have good parking facilities – for example, Penyffordd. It is these factors that make the line popular and give it potential.

After leaving Buckley we start the descent to Deeside. The route we are now on was built as a diversion to provide a more direct line from Buckley to Deeside. The gradient from here is 1 in 53 – all the way down. After passing through an area of woodland and pasture we reach Hawarden. This village is the seat of the Gladstone family, who live at nearby Hawarden Castle. This station is the cleanest on the line, being looked after voluntarily by Mr Bill Roberts, one of our fine senior citizens, who strives to defy the graffiti artists. He received an award for his services from Sir Peter Parker – BR Chairman at the time – who came to Hawarden to present it. We continue downhill, and as we descend keep looking out of the right-hand window and you will be rewarded with spectacular views across Deeside and the North Cheshire Plain. The line passes the housing estates of Aston and arrives at Shotton High Level. Here it is possible to change trains and by walking to Shotton Low Level you can catch trains either to Chester or along the North Wales Coast.

Our train now proceeds across the River Dee on what is the outstanding engineering feature of the line, the Hawarden Bridge. The bridge consists of two bow-shaped fixed spans of 120 feet and a bow-shaped swing span of 285 feet, that weighs 752 tons and was swung hydraulically on one central cylinder. It was the largest of its type in the world, and acclaimed as a fine piece of engineering. The bridge will be celebrating its hundredth birthday in 1989. After crossing the bridge we arrive at Hawarden Bridge Station which serves Shotton steelworks.

After leaving Hawarden Bridge there is a lot to see for the next mile or so. On the right is Dee Marsh Junction where the old connecting curve can still be seen. This was lifted in the dark ages, but the Northgate line still exists and was brought back into use carrying steel coil for Shotton steelworks from Scotland. The line can be seen coming in to join our line as we progress towards Bidston. On the left is the remains of Shotton steelworks. After passing Dee Marsh signal-box of Great Central

A local train crosses Hawarden Bridge. *(Photo:* Rod Fairley)

origin, you can see in the distance the cold-rolling and steel-coating plant — the largest in Europe and still very much in operation. Farther over is the Finnish paper-mill that opened a couple of years ago; there is rail access to the plant. Farther on, on the right, is Deeside Titanium that makes the specialised metal for aircraft.

We now pass into a sandstone cutting that was a sea-wall in ancient times. Just before we enter the cutting, you might catch a glimpse of Shotwick Church on the right. The village had a harbour on the river many moons ago. As we pass through the cutting you might spot Burton Point Station that closed years ago. On emerging from the cutting the line runs along the edge of a slope. On the right are Ness Gardens, botanical gardens owned by Liverpool University, which are well worth a visit. Out of the left-hand window can be seen wonderful views across the Dee Estuary. We now travel along a high embankment as we enter the town of Neston and arrive at Neston Station. This station retains its original buildings although they are in a sorry state. There are moves to try and find a use for these listed buildings to prevent their further deterioration.

On leaving Neston we continue along the embankment, pass through a long cutting, and arrive at Heswall, a busy station with a lot of housing estates near by. The line now passes through another cutting as we start to descend towards the metropolis of Merseyside. On the right is the large housing estate of Woodchurch. The land around here is quite open, on the left is Prenton golf-course and the M53 motorway. As we pass the housing estate a main road passes underneath and just beyond this bridge is the site of what is hoped to be Woodchurch Station, but that is very much still a pipe-dream. After passing the large Ford council estate, we arrive at Upton. We now proceed at a slower pace as we approach the junction with Merseyrail. The land round here has very much gone back to nature, and since the motorway interchange was built has become a wonderful wildlife oasis contrasting enormously with the motorway. When we get the signal to proceed, the train crosses the junction and we enter Bidston Station. This is as far as we can go in the diesel. We now alight and wait for the electric train. When all the passengers for the return journey are aboard and the driver gets the green light, the diesel sets off back to Wrexham. Once the train has cleared the junction, we await the arrival of the electric from West Kirby that will whisk us quickly and quietly to Liverpool.

So there you have it! A journey of variety – the hills of Wales, the beauty of the Dee Estuary, and the pasture-land of West Wirral – 27½ miles across two countries and three counties. And that is why it is known by its rail users' group as the 'Border-line'.

SHREWSBURY–ABERYSTWYTH

by Robert Barton

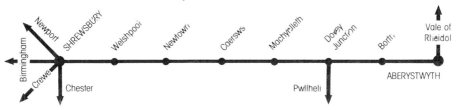

It is said that in Wales there are almost three sheep to each person. If this fact is a true one then the chances are you will see a lot more sheep than people on this wonderful railway journey, which is mostly through Powys, the most sparsely populated county south of the Scottish Border. It is a journey through Wild Wales – where gentle farmland, wide valleys, and black and white inns slowly give way to heather-clad moorland, rushing mountain rivers, and sombre stone cottages.

The route you will be taking is one that, over the centuries, has been trodden by foreign invaders, men seeking war against the English monarchy and, more peacefully, sheep- and cattle-drovers herding their livestock to market. Before the railway reached the area in 1859, ordinary people did not venture far without good reason. The Romans marched into Wales and established forts at places like Caersws; so did the Normans, who built a castle at Montgomery and plundered the Severn Valley. And, in 1485, the Welshman Henry Tudor followed a route not all that different from the one taken by the railway centuries later – from Machynlleth to Newtown, Welshpool, and Shrewsbury – as he gathered the men and arms that were to make him the victorious new king, Henry VII, at the Battle of Bosworth.

The first piece of advice to give all travellers about to journey from Shrewsbury to Mid Wales is to choose a window-seat, from which to enjoy to the full the spectacular scenery which is to come. The train for Machynlleth and Aberystwyth will leave the station by heading south along the Crewe–Cardiff Border Counties line. A hint that we are going on a railway adventure in a different country comes in the form of the gentle strains of the Welsh language being spoken on Shrewsbury Station as people hurry for their seats. A few seconds pass, a couple of stragglers jump on, the door slams – and we're off! At Sutton Bridge Junction the driver picks up the metal token that gives us authority to travel on the single-track route.

We rattle over the points and leave the mainline going down to Hereford and Newport. At first the scenery is of the boring sort popularly associated with railways – dull suburbs, a cemetery, allotments. But this is no *ordinary* rail journey. All of a sudden the view changes and we are in open country – rolling farmland dotted with sheep and we shall see no more suburbs and no more factory chimneys.

Our first 'mountains', appearing on the right, are the Breidden Hills, formed millions of years ago by violent volcanic action. We cross a boundary marked by an insignificant-looking river and are now in Wales. On the left is the Long Mynd, rising to 1,338 feet. It was atop this mountain over 500 years ago, in 1485, that the Welshman Henry Tudor rallied his troops before the last leg of his march into England. In less than two weeks he was to do battle at Bosworth and be crowned King Henry VII on the battlefield.

At Buttington, there is a level crossing and we cross the swiftly flowing River Severn, which we will now hug closely for many miles. Just before the river we cross the site of Offa's Dyke, the national boundary set up by Offa, King of Mercia, over twelve centuries ago.

Coasting along the wide valley, we come to a halt at Welshpool (Y Trallwng), once capital of the ancient province of Powys. Before 1835 the town's official name was Pool or Poole, but there was growing confusion between this and Poole in Dorset, so an Act of Parliament declared that it was henceforth to be called Welshpool! Welshpool is an important market town and the livestock market held here each Monday is one of the longest established in Wales, dating back to the thirteenth century. A building with an interesting tale attached to it is the Grace Evans Cottage in the centre of town. Grace Evans was an ordinary serving-maid but she rescued the Jacobite fifth Earl of Nithsdale from the Tower of London in the eighteenth century. What made the rescue even more impressive was the fact that it took place on the eve of the Earl's expected execution! Grace was presented with the cottage by the Earl for her loyalty. Welshpool is terminus of the 2-foot-6-inch-gauge Welshpool and Llanfair Railway, which enthusiasts have recently reopened into Raven Square in the town itself – previously its terminus was 3 miles out, at Sylfaen.

Leaving the town, look out on the right for a glimpse of Powis Castle, on a hill about ½ mile distant. It has been inhabited continuously for over 500 years.

We cross the River Severn again and climb above it. The countryside is lush and rolling; typical border country in fact. Montgomery Station flashes by. The station is now closed – perhaps the main reason for this being that it was 1½ miles from the town it was supposed to serve. We rejoin the Severn, which is making great, lazy loops below us. To the left, craggy hills rise steeply and we pass through Abermule Station, also now closed and once the junction for a short branch with Kerry which closed in 1931 – on 26 January 1921, the scene of a tragic head-on collision on the single track. The driver of a westbound train had been given the wrong token – the same one that he had just handed in to the signalman. An eastbound train was on its way from Newtown and seventeen people were killed in the ensuing crash. Certain safety precautions were made compulsory after this disaster.

We now run alongside the A483 (on our right) and race the cars. Beyond the road and the river are the remnants of the Montgomeryshire Canal, which reached Newtown in 1821 but was killed off by the railway. A regular canal freight service to Manchester took a leisurely six days and the carriage charge was 2s. 11d. (14½p) per hundredweight!

Newtown (Y Drenewydd) comes next. In 1770 the place was only a village with a population of about 800; then came the era of handloom flannel-weaving and Newtown boomed, its population rising to over 4,000 by 1831. The town's most famous inhabitant was Robert Owen who founded the 'Co-op' – see the museum devoted to him. Newtown's lively market, held in the High Street on Tuesdays and Saturdays, draws bargain-hunters from a wide area. Public transport devotees may be interested to know that the Newtown area was one of the first in Britain to have a post-bus service which was introduced experimentally in 1967.

The hills are now rising to our left – just a hint of what is to come – while to the right the valley opens out, with the river getting lazier and forming little islets. A decaying platform is all that remains of Moat Lane Junction, once a busy interchange point when trains ran south to Builth Wells and Brecon.

Now we cross the Severn for the last time as we swap valleys – from here we will

The Aberystwyth–Euston train slows to pick up token at lonely Talerddig signal-box. (*Photo:* Robert Barton)

be hugging the Afon Garno instead — and pull into Caersws, an attractive little station of grey and white stone. Caersws was an important Roman settlement; the site of a fort is on the right-hand side. In fact, the station itself sits on the site of Roman baths, discovered in 1854. On the left, just before the station, is the course of the Van branch line, which ran to lead-mines at Y Fan, 6 miles distant.

As we leave Caersws, prepare for the most attractive part of the route to Aberystwyth: the section to Cemmaes Road. We will pass towering mountains, hills lined with conifers, isolated stone cottages, and also cross gurgling brooks. It is now more or less a constant climb to the summit of the line at Talerddig — which must have been a tremendous sight in steam days as engines powered noisily towards the coast with heavy express trains.

The climb begins almost immediately. We cross and recross a narrow but rushing Afon Garno, and clatter past a hamlet called Clatter — a name which could so easily have been coined by a poetic Cambrian Railways engineer. More likely it comes from the Welsh *Cletwr* which means 'hard, rough water'. Next comes Carno where the old station is still standing. We pass, on the left, the factory of Laura Ashley, world famous for screen-printed clothes and fabrics.

Our climb comes to an end at Talerddig, 693 feet above sea-level, as the driver exchanges tokens at remote Talerddig signal-box. Now it is downhill all the way to the coast as the train trundles through a 120-foot-deep cutting of solid rock — at the time of its construction it was the world's deepest. Over a stream and then to our left, and far below us opens out the most wonderful vista of a deep mountain valley with cottages strung out along the main road. The railway is high above, clinging to a mountain ledge and picking its way along thickly forested slopes.

Llanbrynmair is the next village, seen to the left, one of some 510 *Llans* throughout

27

Machynlleth. *(Photo:* John R. Edwards)

Wales! (*Llan* originally meant 'enclosure' but then evolved to mean 'church'.) There was once a station here whose down platform was cut in half by the level crossing – a rare if not unique situation in the British Isles.

The railway now noses its way between the hills and over tumbling streams. Sheep munch nonchalantly as our train rushes past. This is Wild Wales at its best. We meet the A489 which will follow us to Machynlleth. Commins Coch (it means 'Red Commons') is a village strung out along the road. Within a couple of miles we reach Cemmaes Road (the signal-box from where we collect the token still spells it in the Anglicised form of Cemmes Road). Look out on your right to spot the route of the old branch line to Dinas Mawddwy, which was closed in 1951.

Our driver's new token will take us the 5 miles to Machynlleth, a fast run alongside the Afon Dyfi. The first glimpse of the Dyfi, on the right, is one of a winding river a long way below. Allow your eyes to lead you beyond, to the grand panorama of mountains and forests stretching to the horizon.

Machynlleth is a major shopping and market town. In the fifteenth century it was the capital of Wales, where the legendary Owain Glyndwr called a parliament. The seal of the local council depicts Owain with a forked beard, holding a sceptre in one hand and an orb in the other. But Machynlleth's best-known 'trademark' is the noble clock-tower at the end of Maengwyn Street, which was presented to the town in 1873 by the Marquess of Londonderry. To the right of the station was the terminus of the Corris Railway, a 2-foot-3-inch-gauge line which served slate quarries to the north. Under the 1858 Act of Parliament that incorporated the line, steam locomotives were not allowed on it – or there would have been a fine of £100 per day! A new Act of 1864 changed all this, though, and steam-engines worked on the line legally until its closure in 1948.

The route from here to Ynyslas is alongside the Afon Dyfi which, like the Severn, is prone to flooding. Navvies who built the line found themselves working in cold and swampy conditions, which made them more unruly than usual. Extra police had to be drafted into the area as a result. In more recent times in January 1976 the line from Dovey Junction to Borth was closed completely for a number of weeks after 'one of the worst storms in living memory'.

28

From Dovey Junction to Ynyslas the train takes us across wind-blown marshland, offering a fine view on the right-hand side of Aberdyfi on the other side of the estuary. To the left, at Ynyslas, we cross a canal-like river, running in a straight line as far as the eye can see. This *is* a canal of sorts; a man-made deviation of the Afon Leri constructed early this century to drain the area in Dutch fashion. The Cambrian Coast Railway to Pwllheli was to have crossed the Dyfi on a viaduct at this point, but marshland was, not surprisingly, found to be an unsuitable foundation. Instead, rail passengers bound for Aberdovey and points north crossed the estuary by ferry until 1867.

Borth, where the train stops momentarily, is a popular holiday village whose 'beach' – Borth Sands – runs for no less than 4 miles and is often used by surfers. Prince Charles surfed here during his time at University College, at Aberystwyth. On the beach near Borth is a 'submerged forest'. These are roots of a pine forest which grew here several thousand years ago when the sea was farther west than it now is.

Without so much as a glimpse of the sea, we head farther inland to avoid some hills and pass the closed stations of Llandre and the intriguingly named Bow Street, now demolished. Then through gently rolling farmland to approach our journey's end from the south-east.

Crowning a hilltop on the left-hand side as we near Aberystwyth is a monument, supposedly an upturned cannon. This was erected by a local landowner to celebrate the Duke of Wellington's victory at the Battle of Waterloo. The monument, it is said, was to have been crowned with the statue of a man on a horse, but unfortunately the money ran out. Soon the narrow-gauge track of the Vale of Rheidol steam-hauled line comes in on the left, and we come to a halt in the seaside resort and university town of Aberystwyth after a fascinating 81-mile run through the centre of Wales.

WELSHPOOL & LLANFAIR LIGHT RAILWAY
by Frank Hastilow

Towards the end of the nineteenth century a number of proposals were put forward for the construction of a railway between the market town of Welshpool and the village of Llanfair Caereinion some 9 miles to the west. The route finally chosen ran from the mainline station at Welshpool and through the town to Raven Square on the outskirts. It then wound its way up the 1 in 30 of Golfa Bank and thence on a somewhat less demanding alignment to Sylfaen and on to Castle Caereinion, the main intermediate station. The line descended into the valley of the River Banwy through Cyfronydd and over a major civil-engineering feature, the bridge over the River Banwy. The railway then reached its terminus at Llanfair Caereinion where there were some basic station buildings and a goods shed.

The railway was opened in 1903 by the Earl of Powys through whose estate part of the line ran. It differs from other Welsh narrow-gauge lines in that it was built to serve the needs of the local agricultural community and not to transport slate down to the sea. It is also built to the unusual gauge – for Britain of 2 feet 6 inches. The two original locomotives, named *Earl* and *Countess* after the Earl and Countess of Powys, were 0-6-0 tank engines built by Beyer Peacock. Shortly after its completion the line was taken over by the Cambrian and that railway was eventually absorbed by the Great Western. As a result the locomotives visited Swindon for overhaul and emerged resplendent with copper-capped chimneys and large brass safety-valve covers – features which they carry to this day.

In 1956 the railway, having passed into BR ownership, was closed although it was still carrying a substantial quantity of freight. The passenger service had ceased some years previously. Its demise was marked by the playing of the 'Dead March' by the Welshpool Town Band at each station in turn.

The preservation society was formed shortly afterwards and managed to lease the line from BR which greatly helped the financial situation at the time. It has since been purchased outright. The section through the town of Welshpool had to be abandoned and the railway now starts from Raven Square, a mile from the BR station. The buildings at Llanfair Caereinion, with substantial additions, have now become the headquarters of the preservation company. The 2 foot 6 inch gauge is unusual and has meant that rolling-stock has had to be acquired from many different sources all over the world. Thus *Countess,* one of the original locomotives, is operating alongside *Sir Drefaldwyn* (Welsh for 'Montgomeryshire'), named thus after coming to the line from the Salzkammergutbahn in Austria though starting its life with the German Army. There are close links also with the Zillertalbahn in Austria and some passenger coaches have been obtained from this source. Thus it is not at all uncommon to see a train of Austrian coaches hauled by an ex-German locomotive wending its way through the Welsh countryside. Another locomotive came from Sierra Leone together with some very impressive coaches built at Gloucester and now returned to this country. Add to these *Joan* from the sugar plantations of the Bahamas, *Monarch* from Bowaters paper-mills in Kent, and the diminutive *Dougal* from a gasworks in Glasgow and it will be seen that the W&L can offer a variety not likely to be seen elsewhere. This together with the beauty of the Welsh countryside in its milder mood makes a visit to the railway an interesting and indeed unique experience.

VALE OF RHEIDOL RAILWAY
by Trevor Garrod

As your diesel train from Shrewsbury completes the final mile into Aberystwyth, you will see on the left and running parallel to it, a narrow-gauge track on which may be puffing a curious little steam tank locomotive pulling a train of diminutive carriages. This is the Vale of Rheidol Railway, opened in 1902, originally to bring ore from lead-mines in the hills down to Aberystwyth Harbour. Passenger services soon followed and today form the only traffic on the 11¾-mile line. The line is operated by British Rail (though there are, at the time of writing, moves to privatise it) and trains run from Easter to October, pulled by one of three steam locomotives and a selection of coaches dating back to the 1920s and 1930s. The gauge is 1 foot 11½ inches, the same as the Ffestiniog Railway farther north. A diesel locomotive was also acquired in 1987.

Nowadays the narrow-gauge train leaves from Aberystwyth mainline station, though it used to have its own separate terminus, and runs out alongside the main-line as far as Llanbadarn, before crossing the River Rheidol and continuing along its valley to Capel Bangor, some 4½ miles from Aberystwyth.

Now the climb begins and our locomotive – *Owain Glyndwr, Llywelyn,* or *Prince of Wales* – can be heard labouring ahead, up a 1 in 50 gradient. Aberffrwd, 7½ miles from Aberystwyth, is 200 feet above sea-level. Locomotives used to pause here to take water, but now do so at the previous station, Nantyronen.

Most of the remaining 4 miles are along a ledge cut in the hillside, with the valley floor way down to the left and a sheer rock face to the right. The train twists its way round curves, ever upwards, with splendid views across the valley of wooded hillsides, the scars of old lead workings, and the Cwm Rheidol power station with its reservoir.

There are two small lineside halts, but most passengers continue to the terminus at Devil's Bridge, in a lovely wooded setting approached through a short rock cutting.

Locomotive No. 8 approaches Devil's Bridge. (*Photo:* Tom Heavyside)

We are now nearly 700 feet above sea-level, and our locomotive runs round the train to prepare for its much easier run back down to the coast.

If you have not just come for the ride (though that in itself is a pleasurable experience), an enjoyable time can be spent up here at Devil's Bridge, walking in the woods, viewing the spectacular Mynach Falls and the deep whirlpool known as the Devil's Punchbowl. You will need to be prepared to clamber up and down a lot of steps and steep pathways to explore it all.

The Devil's Bridge itself is actually three bridges in one, dating back at least 200 years, taking the road over the rapid waters way below. Legend has it that the first bridge ever built across here was constructed by the Devil, on the promise that he would receive the soul of the first living being to cross it. An animal crossed the bridge first, and this so disgusted the Devil that he left, never to return. Visitors to Devil's Bridge probably will wish to return again to this beauty-spot, preferably by train.

MACHYNLLETH–PWLLHELI– THE CAMBRIAN COAST LINE

by Robert Barton

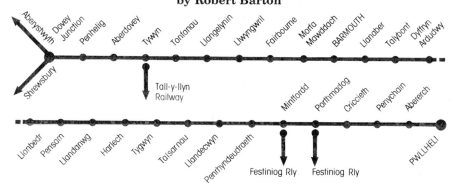

For most of its route it hugs the seashore – along golden beaches, through windswept duneland and, on one dramatic stretch, perched on 100-foot-high cliffs. It carries the traveller to three of the most attractive river estuaries in Wales – the Dyfi, Traeth Bach, and the Mawddach; the last named it cuts straight across on a ½-mile-long viaduct, offering spectacular views. It passes two great castles – in one case right beneath the fortress ramparts. And it explores some of the less-well-known coastal reaches of the Snowdonia National Park.

It was 1863 before the railway was completed along part of the coast to Llwyngwril. Barmouth and Pwllheli were not reached until 1867. The Cambrian Railways Company began promoting the area as a holiday haven almost immediately, though it was not until the 1930s, under the Great Western Railway, that holiday traffic reached a peak. Thankfully, however, the Cambrian Coast never received the garish seaside trappings of, for example, the North Wales Coast and, discounting a few twentieth-century caravan sites you can sit back and enjoy countryside that has changed little over the last hundred years.

The railway journey from Machynlleth to Pwllheli is undoubtedly one of the finest on offer in Britain and the following notes just cannot describe the beauty of this route. Suffice to say that anyone who loves the combination of railways with breath-taking scenery will want to travel this line again and again.

We leave Machynlleth behind and are soon bowling along beside the Afon Dyfi, with the A487 to Aberystwyth on the left. If you can, make sure you are seated on the left-hand side, which offers the best sea and estuary views. Soon we pull into Dovey Junction, an isolated interchange point surrounded by marshland. The signalman here must have one of the loneliest jobs on British Rail. He cannot even drive to work, for the junction is not on a road, so he has to park at Glandyfi a mile distant and then cycle along a footpath. And then he has to cope with 'rush periods' when trains arrive and depart in three directions in a very short space of time, sometimes followed by two hours or more without a single train. This explains why the waiting-room here is 'big enough to hold a dance in' – so that a whole trainload of passengers can be accommodated at once.

We now leave the Aberystwyth line and curve away to the right, clattering over the Afon Dyfi. We are now in the Snowdonia National Park and will stay within its confines, apart for two or three minor excursions, until we cross Traeth Bach near Porthmadog. Now for the first real scenic delights as we trundle along beside the ever-widening Dyfi Estuary, the train constantly winding into little bays and out again round headlands, occasionally diving into short tunnels like a frightened rabbit going into a burrow. It is unlikely we will stop at the halts of Gogarth and Abertafol as they do not serve centres of population, but were built by the Great Western Railway in 1923 and 1933 respectively, along with several other halts, to cater for holiday traffic that never quite developed.

This estuary is a real haven for wildlife. You may be lucky enough to see a buzzard or a kestrel high in the sky, while the soft sands of Dyfi support large numbers of waders – curlews, sandpipers, redshanks, oyster-catchers, and herons – who rummage for small fish and crustaceans. The waters of the estuary are still and mirror-like and, no matter what the weather has been like up till now, the chances are we will meet the sun, its brightness glinting on the sand, as we near the coast.

Into another tunnel and, all of a sudden, the estuary has gone and we find ourselves sandwiched between a road and houses – at rooftop level – at Penhelig. We trundle past the rooftops and plunge into Craig-y-don Tunnel   the longest and the most expensive to build. The railway was to have taken a route round the sea-front, but local opposition forced the engineers to go behind the town of Aberdovey (Aberdyfi) which began life as a small fishing port and was reputed to be a centre for smuggling. Before the railway was built from Dovey Junction, passengers travelling north would cross by ferry from Ynyslas to a station at Aberdovey Harbour, thence continuing their journey by rail on a section cut off from the rest of the rail network. This state of affairs lasted from 1863 until the link-up was completed in 1867, but a branch remained open to Aberdovey Harbour, which grew into quite a busy little port and was visited by graceful sailing-ships. The harbour fell out of use by the late 1920s and is now the promenade. In August 1921 Marconi's yacht *Electra* docked at Aberdovey and one of his first radio messages was broadcast from Tywyn. Many fascinating reminders of Aberdovey as a port can be seen in the Snowdonia National Park Centre, at The Wharf.

Dolgoch on the Talyllyn Railway, near Dolgoch Falls. (*Photo:* Tom Heavyside)

Now turning north, we head past grass-covered sand-dunes that hide the sea. With nothing behind them to give scale they resemble a miniature mountain range. On the right is the terminus of the narrow-gauge Talyllyn Railway, which began a passenger service in 1866. The volunteers of the Talyllyn Railway Preservation Society have been in charge since 1951, and the steam ride to Nant Gwernol is a delightful one. There is a small museum at the terminus which includes an engine built in 1877.

Tywyn is one of the most important stations on our journey: in fact Tywyn has the rare distinction for a town its size of having no less than three railway stations – two are on the Talyllyn. At the time of writing, goods trains on the Cambrian Coast line go no farther north. Tywyn means 'sand dune' and its population of 4,000 expands to over 12,000 in summer with those who come to enjoy its sandy delights. There has been a settlement here since the sixth century, and historians speak of frequent raids on the place during the following 500 years, by warriors from Ireland and Scandinavia. In St Cadfan's Church is the 7-foot-tall St Cadfan's Stone, dating from about the seventh century, which is believed to bear the oldest Welsh writing in existence.

Leaving Tywyn we find the sea at last, the grey waters of Cardigan Bay unrolling towards Ireland. We cross the narrow estuary of the Afon Dysynni and speed through Tonfanau where an old army camp lies deserted and rotting, like a ghost town. The camp came to life in 1972, however, when it was used as a temporary base for hundreds of expelled Ugandan Asians – all of whom arrived in a special from Anglesey, but not before they had endured over twenty hours' isolation in the blizzard-stricken train.

Our train climbs steadily now following the coastline, and directly ahead and to the left is a wonderful vista of sea and mountain. To the right, drystone walls transform the fields into a veritable jigsaw puzzle. Also on the right is Llangelynin, another GWR pausing-place, opened in 1930. With its smart blue and cream shelter and sawtooth valancing, it looks like something straight out of a model railway. Above the line here, to the right though it cannot easily be seen, is Llangelynin Church. In its isolated location high on the cliff-top, it must be one of the most beautifully sited churches in Wales – but no place in which to worship during a westerly gale, I am sure. The church dates from the seventh century and is dedicated to St Celynin. Near the entrance is the grave of Abram Wood 'a travelling gypsy buried 13th December, 1799'. Inside the church is what is possibly the only double horse-bier in existence. This strange contraption, pulled by two horses, was used to carry coffins from remote hill farms in the area: many a Welsh farmer would make his final journey along narrow mountain paths in this way.

Now the train begins the steep descent to Llwyngwril which, with Machynlleth, must be the most difficult to pronounce place-name on the line. A phonetic approximation is 'Loo-in-gooril' but, no matter how you say it, a Welshman will always correct you. Rail enthusiasts will note that it is the only station with the magical consecutive letters G-W-R in its name. The signal-box and passing loop here closed in 1972, which is the explanation for the strange dog-leg curve our train swings through. Now one token has to suffice for the 14½-mile stretch from Tywyn to Barmouth.

Llwyngwril is a pretty village whose focal point is a very old stone bridge spanning a thickly wooded and fast-flowing Afon Gwril. Just beyond the bridge the main road bends sharply and stone cottages and a whitewashed hotel are attractively juxtaposed.

Beyond Llwyngwril prepare for a breath-taking cliff-top ride. Few railways can compete with this – anywhere. We climb steadily, hugging the shoreline, and trundling over a foaming waterfall slow down to the regulation speed of 15 m.p.h.

Soon we are on a narrow cliff ledge 100 feet above the crashing waves of Cardigan Bay. Seagulls cry and wheel in anger – this is *their* domain!

These are the Friog Cliffs (*Friog* means a 'place of brambles'; 'high land'). They were the scene of two tragic accidents, one in 1883 and the other in 1933. In both cases, debris crashed down the mountainside and the train-drivers and firemen were sent to their deaths on the rocks below. Also in both cases, though, the carriages carrying passengers remained safely on the rails. To ensure an accident would never happen here again, a concrete protection canopy was built on the cliffs in 1933. I would like to think of it as a monument to the railwaymen who died – it is certainly a graceful structure – and our train passes slowly through it. To underline the fact that this stretch is completely safe today, British Rail report that some £200,000 was spent as recently as 1975 on reinforcing sections of cliff eroded by the restless sea.

To the right of our train the mass of the mountain Cader Idris rises above, reaching 2,927 feet. The name means 'Chair of Idris', the giant, and legend says that whoever spends a night on the summit will return the following morning either a poet – or a madman.

The cruise down to the resort of Fairbourne is like a gentle landing in an aeroplane. And there is some fine scenery to the port (left-hand) side: the curving sweep of Fairbourne Bay, the town of Barmouth across the estuary, and a wonderful view of the coast will follow, backed by the mountains of Snowdonia. The concrete defences seen along Fairbourne beach were built as a precaution against seaborne invasion during the Second World War.

Fairbourne (change here for the Fairbourne Miniature Railway) was an artificially created resort, built by the McDougal Estate. Its name was, by local request, to have been Ynysfaig but neither the developers nor the railway were keen on that. Fairbourne Station was one of several sites on the Cambrian Coast line to have a 'Camping Coach' introduced by the GWR in 1934. This was a permanently sited

Sprinter crosses Barmouth Bridge with Cader Idris in the background. (*Photo:* Robert Barton)

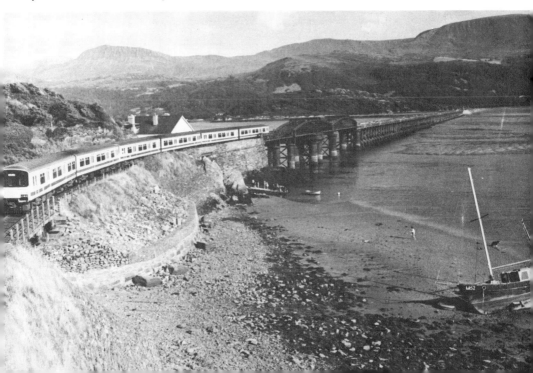

carriage that people could hire for a self-catering holiday. These coaches' Indian summer ended in 1972, however, when they were removed or broken up.

Morfa Mawddach comes next, which until 1960 was named Barmouth Junction. The trackbed of the former line to Dolgellau, Bala, and Ruabon, closed completely in 1965, can be seen curving away to the right immediately beyond the halt. This is now a pleasant walkway for 6 miles of the route along the River Mawddach, to Penmaenpool. The large station building and signal-boxes have now been demolished, so little of the past remains here, but L. J. Vaughton, who has lived most of his life near the junction, remembers when it was a very busy place, alive with passengers and steam-engines. The station refreshment room doubled as the local pub, and railway staff and local people would down their drinks and join in some hearty Welsh singing — the melodic sounds drifting across the otherwise silent estuary.

We now begin to cross the Mawddach Estuary upon the magnificent Barmouth Bridge. Nearly ½ mile in length, this is the longest timber trestle bridge remaining in Wales, and is certainly one of the high spots of our journey. The bridge consists of 113 timber spans and two long steel ones — one of these revolves to allow tall ships to pass and this still happens occasionally.

We come to a stop at Barmouth, the major intermediate station between Machynlleth and Pwllheli. Its original name was Abermawddach ('Mouth of the Mawddach') but this was corrupted into Abermaw, thence into Bermo, which was Anglicised into Barmouth. The place was a busy little port from Tudor times — its principal trade came from the export of 'webs', a type of coarse woollen cloth woven by cottagers and farmers in the locality. But the old sailing-ships also used to load up with copper, timber, and slate. The arrival of the railway in the 1860s quickly killed the port and Barmouth was soon transformed into a popular Victorian seaside resort, easily reached by train from the Midlands.

To the right, above the station, is St John's Church. This sturdy looking structure had just been completed in 1892 when the tower collapsed — an unfortunate incident which involved another six years' work. A path leads past the church to Dinas Oleu, the first property owned by the National Trust. The climb is well worth while, giving the visitor a bird's-eye view of the town. Also recommended, if you have time, is the Panorama Walk above the waters of the Mawddach Estuary.

Out of Barmouth, and our train is soon bowling along the coast again. We pass Llanaber: the sturdy sea-wall that the train runs along was built after terrific storms washed away long sections of track in 1922. Extensive maintenance of these sea defences is required at frequent intervals to keep them in good order. Just over 2 miles farther on is Talybont, serving the pretty stone-built village, and a little over a mile beyond here we pull into Dyffryn Ardudwy. During GWR days the station was named Dyffryn-on-Sea — a title that would not be tolerated today under the Trade Descriptions Act, for the sea is over a mile away. Near Dyffryn are a number of Stone Age burial chambers dating from about 3000 BC.

Llanbedr is next. To the left, about a mile away, is Mochras or Shell Island, famed for the dozens of varieties of shells found on its sands. It is reached by a causeway at low tide and some years ago the place caused a stir as an unofficial nudist camp. To the right, the lane leads to the village of Llanbedr, where cottages of solid grey stone are collected together around a bridge and stream. Also besides the stream is the Victoria Inn, a traditional and cosy pub with an especially welcome roaring fire in the winter. The Maes Artro Craft Village is about 100 yards south of Llanbedr — it includes craft shops, an aquarium, and an adventure playground.

As we pull into Pensarn we cross the wide Afon Atro at a point where there used to be a small harbour used by coastal trading ships. Rotting timbers in the estuary here are said to belong to a vessel two men took to America with a cargo of slate. On their return they went to a pub, where they had a fierce argument. In his rage

A Sprinter at Harlech under the shadow of the castle. *(Photo:* Robert Barton)

one of the men returned to the ship and set fire to it. On the left is the Llanbedr military airfield which sends up pilotless aircraft that tow targets to be shot down by fighters or missiles being put through their paces by the Ministry of Defence.

It is barely ½ mile to the next halt, Llandanwg. As we arrive, look out on the left for fifteenth-century St Tanwg's Church, unusual in that it is almost completely buried in the sand-dunes. The church is not often used and one day the dunes may totally engulf it. There has probably been a church on this site since the sixth century.

We rejoin the sea and there is a fantastic view of the shoreline curving round to the Lleyn Peninsula — our destination, Pwllheli, is somewhere along there. Cutting inland, the famous Royal St David golf-course is on the left, while straight ahead is the imposing structure of Harlech Castle.

Harlech Station is directly beneath the castle's massive walls. The land now occupied by the station was once under water, for the castle rock was lapped by Cardigan Bay before the sea receded. One of many castles built by Edward I in the thirteenth century, as part of his scheme to subdue the unruly Welsh, Harlech was constructed by a force of 800 men. It was captured by the Welsh prince Owain Glyndwr in 1404 but by Elizabethan times it was little more than a debtors' prison. The famous march 'Men of Harlech' was inspired by the brave but vain attempt to defend the castle in 1468 during the Wars of the Roses.

At Harlech the driver collects a new token to take us through to Porthmadog. We head across the flat landscape of Morfa Harlech (*Morfa* means 'Sea-edge land') and come to Tygwyn. Mountains to the right, though they look uninviting, were the site of primitive habitation thousands of years ago. There are stone circles, a fort, and a dozen or more standing stones that mark the route of a Bronze Age trackway.

To the left, across the still waters of Traeth Bach ('Beach on the river-bend') is an unusual white village nestling among trees. It is not the sort of hamlet you normally expect to see in Wales — nor in Britain for that matter. This is Portmeirion, a unique fantasy village created by the architect Sir Clough Williams-Ellis (1883–1978), who literally 'collected' interesting buildings from different parts of the country and rebuilt them here. The TV series of the 1960s, *The Prisoner* starring Patrick McGoohan, was filmed on location here. Sir Clough, incidentally, always looked on the railway with affection and had many friends among the line's employees when it was still known as the Cambrian Railways Company. We come to Talsarnau ('End of the causeways'), a name derived from the fact that a causeway ran down to the estuary. The station is in the middle of an area that was reclaimed from the sea in the early nineteenth century by the building of embankments. Without this reclamation, neither the railway nor the road would have been able to follow its present course and Talsarnau itself would never have grown from a solitary farm to the village seen on the right-hand side.

Mountains are rising up all around us as we make for Llandecwyn. In the range to the right lies a small lake used as a reservoir for Porthmadog, which has a gruesome legend dating back to the seventeenth century. An old woman named Dorti was suspected of witchcraft and as a punishment she was rolled down the hills to Llandecwyn in a spiked barrel. A place thought to be her grave is marked by a large chunk of quartz-rock which, in those superstitious times, was thought to stop the witch's ghost from haunting the locality.

We cross the Afon Dwyryd on a curving trestle bridge which doubles as a road toll-bridge – thus saving motorists a 7½-mile detour via Maentwrog. On the right is an explosives factory, part of ICI, its buildings spread out over the mountainside as a safety measure. Until April 1980, special freight workings which provided all year round traffic on the Cambrian originated here, but now the goods begin their journey by road as far as Blaenau Ffestiniog.

Penrhyndeudraeth means 'The headland between two beaches' and before reclamation took place less than two centuries ago the place was little more than a swamp. The route from here up to Minffordd is a steep and sharply curved one and, during steam days, banking engines would assist heavy trains from Penrhyndeudraeth through to Criccieth. Our climbing train offers an excellent view of the estuary, mountains, and the route we have just travelled, glimpsed through a veil of trees.

At Minffordd the Ffestiniog Railway passes above us, and this is a useful interchange point, or you may prefer to join the Ffestiniog at the line's terminus, Porthmadog. Whatever you do, it is a worthwhile journey: especially now that the trains run all the way to Blaenau Ffestiniog, where they link up with the Conwy Valley line of BR, which runs to Betws-y-Coed and Llandudno.

Now there is a wonderful view, to the right, along the Afon Glaslyn to the highest mountains of Snowdonia. On the left cars can be seen negotiating the causeway known as The Cob (also shared by the Ffestiniog Railway) created in the nineteenth century by William Alexander Maddocks, MP, who reclaimed 7,000 acres of land in the process. Directly ahead is the distinctive mountain Moel-y-Gest which at 861 feet stands sentinel above the harbour town of Porthmadog. Today the harbour is little more than a mooring place for pleasure-boats but for over a century it was one of the most important on the Welsh coast, responsible for the transhipment of slate, brought down from the mountains by the Ffestiniog Railway, to distant corners of the world. On the right-hand side just before we enter the station is the terminus of the Welsh Highland Railway, another narrow-gauge line, which originally ran up the Aberglaslyn Pass to Beddgelert and beyond. In 1980 enthusiasts succeeded in reopening a short stretch to Pen-y-Mount.

Leaving Porthmadog (with the final token to take us through to Pwllheli) we pass Tremadog, nestling at the foot of a mountain to the right. T. E. Lawrence, better known as 'Lawrence of Arabia', was born here in 1888. A little farther on is Wern, where there was a busy railway goods depot until 1957: Wern Siding, as it was called, was once one of the busiest places on the line, always echoing to the sound of steam-engines.

We cross marshland and, to the right, a lone chapel can be seen with no other buildings for company. This is the Chapel of Ynyscynhaearn, the resting-place of composer David Owen (1712–41) who wrote the air 'David of the White Rock' as played by the Welsh Guards. The line curves to the right and we meet the sea at Black Rock Sands for a lovely run along the beach to Criccieth. This town is dominated by its castle, rebuilt by Edward I. Scorch marks on the walls and stones split by fire-heat are reminders of Owain Glyndwr's successful capture of the castle in 1404. It is, of course, Lloyd George's home town and numerous reminders of the great man abound in and around the area.

Our train continues westwards and is soon running along a solid sea-wall built by the GWR after storms breached the track in 1922. This is another place where the sea defences need constant attention in winter. We speed past the site of Afon Wen – only a weed-ridden platform remains to remind us that this was once a busy junction where trainloads of people, luggage, and goods would change or be carted over to trains going north to Caernarfon, Bangor, and beyond. This line, and the wind-swept junction, were both closed in December 1964.

After about ½ mile we pass through the centre of Butlin's Pwllheli Holiday Camp and, in summer, are treated to a view of holiday-makers enjoying themselves on the boating-pool or in the fair-ground. This holiday centre started life as a training-camp for the Navy during the Second World War. Penychain is conveniently situated for the patrons of Butlin's.

Abererch is next and soon we are slowing down for journey's end. The train runs along the edge of the harbour and we arrive at Pwllheli, 58 miles from Machynlleth and 118½ miles from Shrewsbury. Pwllheli is the main centre and market town for

Pwllheli.

the Lleyn Peninsula, and every Wednesday a large market consisting of some 200 stalls is held.

In the latter part of the nineteenth century the ambitious Cambrian Railways Company had plans to extend the line northwards to Porth Dinllaen. In the event the scheme never got off the ground but we should be grateful that the railway promoters got as far as they did, for in doing so they opened up a line that is scenically beyond comparison.

Note

These two articles by Robert Barton originally appeared in *Cambrian Rail,* published by the Cambrian Coast Line Action Group, in 1982, and are reprinted here in slightly abridged form by kind permission of the author.

During 1988, radio signalling is being introduced on the routes, with a control centre at Machynlleth.

GLOUCESTER–NEWPORT

by John Powell

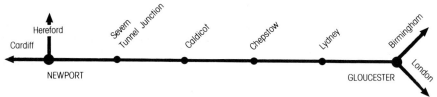

The present station at Gloucester is a revamped layout of the former Great Western Central Station. The only recognisable parts of the old station today are the buildings on Platform 4. Though officially divided between Platforms 1 and 2, the main platform on the southern side is arguably the longest in Britain. Gloucester's former London Midland & Scottish station at Eastgate disappeared under an office block and superstore several years ago.

As the train leaves the station, there is a good view of the Cathedral and city centre to the left. After crossing the inner ring road, the railway passes over the east channel of the River Severn on to Alney Island. The single-track Docks branch comes in from the left before we cross the west river channel. Between the railway bridge and the new A40 road bridge to the right, lies the old road bridge, which since becoming disused has sagged several inches in the middle. The site of Over Junction from where a line once ran to Ledbury is still marked by a BR notice-board.

Travelling west, the spire of Highnam Parish Church to the right is a prominent landmark before the line passes under the Gloucester to Chepstow road. At the next road bridge the site of Oakle Street Station is passed, then, after two gated level crossings, comes Grange Court. There is now only a loop line in each direction plus crossovers of what used to be a junction station for a line to Hereford via Longhope and Ross-on-Wye. Passing near Westbury-on-Severn, the line proceeds to Newnham, giving good views of the River Severn *en route*. Newnham used to have a station, too, and may do so again one day.

Passing through Newnham Tunnel and over the main road, the line passes an area of fairly flat scrubland. This is all that remains of the once-important sidings, docks, and branch-line junctions of Bullo Pill. At the western end of this area lies the slope down to the now-closed docks on the left, and the embankment of the former Cinderford branch which closed to passengers in 1957. It was also around this point that the first attempt was made, in about 1820, to tunnel under the river. However, the workings became flooded and were abandoned.

As the line moves away from the Severn, we plunge into what is for much of the year, a 'green tunnel', after which comes the site of the long-gone Awre Junction, although the former signal-box still stands.

Passing a speed restriction board on the left, the line meets the River Severn, and remains in close proximity to it for several miles. From this point, a round, turret-like object is visible standing above the opposite bank, with a bridge abutment immediately behind it. This is all that remains of the former Severn railway bridge, which although only single-track saw good service for both the Severn & Wye Railway and the Great Western Railway. It passed into the possession of British Rail and continued in use until the early 1960s, when several of a convoy of oil barges struck the bridge supports one foggy night while trying to find the entrance to the Gloucester & Sharpness Canal. The bridge was seriously damaged, and although rebuilding it was considered it was eventually demolished.

Following a brief detour inland, the embankment which carried the railway line up to the bridge can be clearly seen. Bearing away from the river, the train approaches Lydney. The present station − formerly Lydney Junction − is but a shadow of its former self, with just a shelter on each platform, and a loop line in each direction, plus the remains of a rarely used goods yard. The spire of Lydney Parish Church is visible beyond the yard.

A few miles north of Lydney is the private Dean Forest Railway at Norchard. This was originally part of the Sharpness–Lydney–Cinderford–Lydbrook line. The Lydney–Parkend section some 5 miles long is all that now remains. Since the closure of Lydney Town Station, the present station has been rather isolated from the town centre. However, there are now plans to introduce a bus link.

From Lydney, we cross the River Lyd and the adjacent canal, before passing through fairly flat country, broken by the occasional cutting. Between Lydney and Chepstow, Berkeley and Oldbury nuclear power-stations can be seen on the far bank of the estuary. Berkeley power-station is a square-towered set of buildings opposite Lydney, while Oldbury power-station is a more rounded collection of buildings, roughly midway between the two towns. In the distance can be seen the Severn road bridge.

Tidenham limestone quarry can be seen to the right. It is rail-served by the remains of the Chepstow to Monmouth Wye Valley line, which joins us from the right in the following cutting. This cutting takes us through the rock outcrop immediately before the River Wye, and the Welsh border. Emerging from the hillside, we cross the river on Isambard Kingdom Brunel's bridge, and to the right is a new road bridge (part of the Chepstow bypass) and beyond that, John Rennies's road bridge of 1816. Before the railway bridge was built, trains used to terminate on each side and passengers were conveyed across the road bridge between the two stations by horse-drawn coach.

Chepstow's most famous landmark is, of course, the castle. This is clearly visible from the train as it crosses the rail bridge. It has guarded this strategic route into Wales since soon after the Norman Conquest, and was still in use as late as the seventeenth century.

Chepstow Station has very long platforms which are not really warranted by the train service nowadays except, possibly, by the once-daily High Speed Train. The town centre is a short walk from the station, and still possesses most of its medieval town walls. In addition to the castle, there is a museum housed in the former town hospital on the opposite side of Bridge Street. Chepstow has the largest racecourse in Wales, and 5 miles up the Wye Valley is the famous Tintern Abbey in its dramatic setting. A two-hourly bus service operates from Chepstow to Tintern.

Leaving Chepstow, the train enters a cutting, with glimpses of the River Wye through gaps in the rock outcrop to the left. Bearing to the right, we pass under the Wye Bridge, adjoining the Severn road bridge carrying the M4 motorway into Wales.

From here to the outskirts of Newport the land is fairly flat, again with only the occasional cutting to break the monotony. Passing Mathern Marina on the left, we next reach Portskewett with its disused platforms and footbridge still intact. The freight branches to Sudbrook and the Dinham Ministry of Defence establishment converge from either side to meet us at Caldicot Junction, and we approach Caldicot Halt. Despite the primitive appearance of the station, Caldicot sees considerable commuter traffic, mainly to Newport and Cardiff. The town is notable for its castle, about a mile from the station.

Beyond Caldicot, we approach Severn Tunnel Junction. To the right is a deep cutting, carrying the lines up from the Severn Tunnel. At just over 4 miles in length, the tunnel is the longest of its kind in Britain. It carries the lines from London Paddington and Bristol under the Severn Estuary and into Wales. High Speed Trains from London reach the tunnel in just under one and a half hours.

Having celebrated its centenary in 1986, the Severn Tunnel is as busy today as ever it was. Its construction was a long and costly undertaking, both financially and in human lives. Most of the work was done by pick and shovel, and with primitive dynamite. At one stage there was a serious setback when an underground river was struck and the workings were flooded. To this day, the river still runs into the tunnel, and a pumping-station at Sudbrook removes huge volumes of water. Once driven by Cornish beam-engines, the pumps were converted to electric operation in the 1960s.

The lines from Gloucester and the tunnel join at the aptly named Severn Tunnel Junction Station. Once boasting links with most parts of the country, with many express trains calling there, it now handles only local traffic apart from the occasional train to the South Coast. Three of the four platforms are used by passenger trains. The one farthest to the right led into the diesel depot before this closed in 1987. Severn Tunnel Junction used to be a hive of freight activity, with its two 'hump-shunting' yards, one at each side of the line. The yard on the left closed a long while ago, and the remaining traffic from the other yard has now been transferred to Newport.

From Severn Tunnel Junction, the two-track line becomes four-track. Passing Undy and Magor villages on the right, we pass under the concrete Bishton Flyover which carries one of the relief lines over the main lines, so that both are now to our left. The reason is soon apparent as Llanwern steelworks loom up on the left and dominate the landscape for the next 3 miles, as far as the outskirts of Newport. There is a great deal of freight traffic to and from the steelworks which can enter or leave by rail connections to the relief lines at both ends. The urban sprawl of Newport appears to the right, and after we pass Liswerry Pond the Uskmouth freight branch line comes in from the left, heralding the start of East Usk yard on the same side. Shortly Maindee East and West Junctions are passed, both on the right, and we cross the tidal River Usk parallel to a road bridge to the left. Also on the left, wedged between the Old Green interchange and the river can be seen the ruins of Newport Castle, as we approach the station.

NEWPORT

by Adrian Fawcett

Newport is a busy industrial and commercial centre, with a population of approximately 135,000. Once a thriving port, the docks see relatively little traffic nowadays and the network of freight railway lines and marshalling yards have largely disappeared.

There are good shopping centres in Commercial Street and John Frost Square, and then there is the recently opened Kingsway Centre. Another shopping complex is planned for the near future. Also recently completed is the Newport Centre, a leisure centre situated between Kingsway and the River Usk.

Newport's main historical claim to fame is that it was the scene of the Chartist Riots in 1839. The story is told in mosaic at John Frost Square, and in the museum at the opposite end of the square.

At the top of Stow Hill is situated Newport Cathedral, a much-enlarged Norman building. It is unusually dedicated to St Gwynllyw, now corrupted to St Woolos, and the cathedral possesses the only ring of twelve bells in Wales.

An unusual feature of Newport is its transporter bridge, opened in 1906, and standing 242 feet above the Usk. It is one of only two such bridges in Britain (the other is at Middlesbrough) and consists of a massive steel gantry, supporting a movable platform which carries vehicles across the river. However, the bridge has been out of action for several years and is awaiting repairs expected to cost £2,500,000.

On the outskirts of Newport is Tredegar House and Country Park, formerly the home of the Morgans of Tredegar. The house dates mainly from the seventeenth century, and guided tours take place in summer. The grounds are open all the year round. Bus routes 3 and 15 run from the bus station (five minutes' walk from the railway station) to Duffryn, close by Tredegar House.

Caerleon

Three miles north-east of Newport is the small town of Caerleon, site of the Roman town and legionary fortress of Isca Silurum, established in AD 75. The remains open to the public include the amphitheatre, baths, and fragments of the barracks. There is also a Roman Legionary Museum. This pleasant dormitory town for Newport is well worth a visit and can be reached by bus – Nos 2 or 7 from Newport bus station.

NEWPORT–SHREWSBURY
by Tim Young and Adrian Fawcett

The Newport to Shrewsbury line, marketed by British Rail as The Marches Line, runs for most of its 94 miles through pleasant rural countryside close to the England/Wales border. Despite being the principal route from South Wales to the North-West and North Wales, the line was gradually downgraded from mainline status and at one stage the Hereford–Shrewsbury section of the line was rumoured to be a candidate for closure. In the last few years, however, the fortunes of the line have improved dramatically, and it is due to have an hourly Sprinter service throughout its length from May 1988.

Our train, which probably started its journey at Cardiff Central Station, leaves from Newport's Platform 3, and crosses the main Newport to Abergavenny road, then the River Usk before curving away from the London line along the western side of the Maindee Triangle. After passing under the M4 motorway we re-cross the River Usk before following the west bank as far as Caerleon. Caerleon is claimed to be the

Cardiff-Crewe train near Caerleon. (*Photo:* Tom Heavyside)

home of King Arthur's legendary Round Table, and also possesses substantial Roman remains. The station closed in 1962, but see Newport on page 43 for details of bus services.

The railway curves to the left, and follows the valley of the small Afon Llwyd. From here to the summit at Pontypool, we climb steadily at gradients of up to 1 in 95. Burton's biscuit factory is passed on the left, the site of Llantarnam Station. Then comes Llantarnam Junction, which has been totally obliterated since the freight-only line to Blaenavon disappeared in 1982. There are factories to the left and parkland to the right as we approach Cwmbran Station, opened in May 1986.

Cwmbran is a New Town which now has a population of nearly 50,000. Cwmbran Stadium is at times host to major international athletics events, and the town centre which takes the form of a very large pedestrian precinct is just a few minutes' walk from the station.

Proceeding north, the train soon passes Pilkington's fibreglass plant and Panteg steelworks – the blue buildings to the left. The tall grey chimney of the controversial Rechem chemical incinerator can be seen to the right. The level ground we now pass and which is crossed by the main road, was once the site of Pontypool's extensive locomotive sheds and a network of railway tracks. Pontypool Station is a shadow of its former self. Its large island platform, now almost completely bare, used to be even longer with a bay platform at each end. Known then as Pontypool Road, for the town had two other central stations, it was an important railway junction. Today Pontypool Station is little more than a wayside halt, a mile from the town centre.

In the eighteenth century, Pontypool was an important industrial centre. This was largely due to the innovative Hanbury family who, among other things, were the first people to successfully manufacture tin. The fascinating industrial history of the area is described in the Valley Inheritance Centre, a museum situated in the very extensive Pontypool Park which also contains a leisure centre and artificial ski slope.

After Pontypool the landscape changes, becoming mainly pastoral with the occasional farmhouse or cottage; on one side a mountain ridge, to the other the Usk again. The dual carriageway which appears by our side heralds our arrival at Abergavenny. The station is an old building in attractive pink stone, and Abergavenny itself is a flourishing market town which forms a good base for walking in the surrounding mountains. Abergavenny Castle made history in 1176 when the Norman knight William De Braose invited the Welsh Lords of Gwent as guests at Christmas and, while they were disarmed, murdered them all.

Our train climbs again from Abergavenny to a summit at Llanvihangel, the highest point between Newport and Hereford. On the way up, you cannot fail to notice the 1,955-foot-high conical-shaped Sugar Loaf Mountain to the left with Skirrid Fawr to the right. The latter, standing at 1,601 feet, is also known as the Holy Mountain because it suffered a great landslip many years ago and legend has it that this landslip occurred on the day of the Crucifixion. After the summit at Llanvihangel the train heads north-east and makes a beeline for the Wales/England border at Pontrilas. There is nothing to mark this international boundary, but Pontrilas will be clearly recognised even as you pass through at speed by the small church set on top of a conical hill on your left, followed by Pontrilas sawmills whose green buildings have the name of the firm prominently displayed on their roofs. The trackbed of the former branch line to Hay-on-Wye can be seen curving away to the left.

For the next 10 miles or so, just sit back in your seat and enjoy the superb Herefordshire countryside, with its cider orchards.

As we approach Hereford, the square tower of the Cathedral will be seen to the left, although at the time of writing it was shrouded in scaffolding as part of a restoration project. It dates from the eleventh century and contains a number of treasures, including the oldest map in the world known as the 'Mappa Mundi', and

Hereford Cathedral.

a chained library. This historic town is well worth exploring, but the approaches from the station are not attractive.

Hereford and the nearby Malvern Hills were home to Sir Edward Elgar whose music is celebrated and performed each year at the Three Choirs Festival held in turn at the cathedrals of Hereford, Worcester, and Gloucester.

H. P. Bulmer, PLC, local cider manufacturers, have established a steam railway centre in Hereford and some of their locomotives are often 'borrowed' by British Rail to run ever-popular steam-hauled specials, particularly on the line on which we are travelling.

Hereford Station is a substantial building, with two through tracks for trains not requiring to stop. It also has some attractive flower-beds on the platforms.

Soon after leaving Hereford, the single-track line to Malvern, Worcester, and Birmingham curves away to the right at Shelwick Junction. Running beside the small River Lugg, we come to sidings and a short branch line for freight trains, at Moreton on Lugg. Shortly after, the two lines separate by a few yards for the parallel single-track Dinmore Tunnels, and on emerging we see the village of Hope under Dinmore nestling at the foot of the hill we have just passed through, on our right. Soon we speed across Marlbrook level crossing, then slow as we arrive at the attractive little station of Leominster.

Leofric was said to have founded Leominster, though this claim to fame does not appear to have been so well documented or known, compared to the one notorious exploit of his wife, which every schoolboy can recount in graphic detail. Her name? Lady Godiva! Look out, too, for the black and white timbered buildings which are comparatively prevalent in this area.

Continuing north, we pass into Shropshire at Woofferton Junction. It has not actually been a junction since the line to Tenbury Wells was closed, but the signal-box there still bears the name. From Woofferton we follow the River Teme on which Ludlow is situated. Shortly before we arrive in the town, the train crosses the Ludlow bypass, and the Parish Church of St Lawrence may be seen to the left. Ludlow is arguably the finest historic town on the Marches, and from Norman times until the Civil Wars the Welsh Borders were governed from here. The fine castle was probably founded during the reign of Henry I.

The station, which is not staffed, comes immediately after the very short Ludlow Tunnel. On leaving Ludlow we go under the bypass and on our right catch a glimpse of the town's racecourse. The River Onny, a tributary of the Teme, and the A49 keep us company to Craven Arms — the railway crosses both at Onibury. On our right we pass Stokesay Castle, which is still inhabited, and a single line curves in from the left bringing the Heart of Wales line in to join us before our train runs into Craven Arms Station, formerly known as Craven Arms and Stokesay. During the Second World War a secret train was kept under wraps in sidings here ready to be used as a mobile control room for the whole rail network, should it be needed. It was only removed a few years ago. Craven Arms took its name from a nearby coaching inn.

The scenery dramatically changes as we wend our way through the valley between the Long Mynd on our left and the spectacular Wenlock Edge on our right. The next station, at Church Stretton, serves the three Stretton villages, Little Stretton, Church Stretton, and All Stretton. There used to be railway halts which served these other two villages as well. The hills stay with us as we descend from the highest point on the line at Church Stretton, through the villages of Leebotwood, Dorrington, and Condover, to the Severn Valley at Shrewsbury.

As we approach Shrewsbury a single line trails in from the left, which is the Mid Wales line to Aberystwyth and Pwllheli. The attractive square-built red-brick abbey church can shortly be seen to our right, while beyond is the 133-foot-6-inches-high column, the tallest Greek Doric column in the world, and the town's grateful tribute to one of its bravest sons, Lord Rowland Hill, who was the Duke of Wellington's right-hand man. The town centre can be seen to our left in the distance beyond the stands of Gay Meadow, Shrewsbury Town's football ground.

Our train now passes a huge triangular railway junction, the other two sides connecting to the Wolverhampton line. In the middle is a long tall signal-box, which looks very impressive as it towers above passing trains. It now also has the distinction of possessing the largest surviving mechanical lever frame in Britain. As we approach the station, the first parts of the platforms are directly over the River Severn. Shrewsbury Station has recently had its ticket-office completely rebuilt with a new travel centre, too. The architects have done a superb job and the station is still in keeping with the architecture of the historic buildings surrounding it.

Shrewsbury Castle overlooks the station and river, and is open to the public. There is plenty more of interest in the town which is surrounded on three sides by the Severn. At opposite sides are the historic English and Welsh bridges. Shrewsbury also has an excellent selection of shops and a large indoor market. It was also the birthplace of Charles Darwin in 1809, renowned for his book *The Origin of Species*, expounding his theory of evolution through natural selection, which even today is generally accepted as correct, though doubts have recently been cast.

HEART OF WALES LINE
by Mike Watson

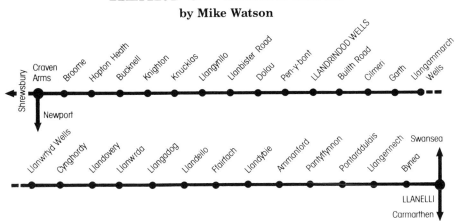

The Heart of Wales line is a fascinating railway. A checklist of its attractions includes: the route of one of the oldest Welsh standard-gauge railways; the highest standard-gauge railway summit in Wales; Britain's longest single-track section without a passing loop; the longest 'light railway' in the country; and, above all, some of the most beautiful scenery in England and Wales. And yet its trains are not forever crowded out with tourists – a journey along it is one of the most relaxing ways of seeing Mid Wales at its best.

The route today is the legacy of no less than five early railway companies. But it was the London & North Western Railway – the 'Premier Line' – which brought them together to form an artery by which it could tap the industries of the south-west Wales coalfields.

The Heart of Wales line as it is properly called begins its south-westerly course at Craven Arms, where it diverges from the Crewe–Cardiff mainline. All trains on the line, however, run to and from Shrewsbury, some 19½ miles to the north.

At Craven Arms crossing signal-box, the train-driver will receive the single-line token: the section to Llandrindod Wells is the longest in the country without a passing loop, and considerably restricts the line's capacity. The train then crosses to the up line before negotiating Central Wales Junction at the south end of the station.

Stokesay Castle lies a little way down the mainline, and nearer to the station are the auction rings of the local livestock market. But Craven Arms, taking its name from the local public house, was basically a railway town – a Crewe or Swindon on a much smaller scale.

After the first of many request halts at Broome, the line undulates towards Hopton Heath, leaving to the left Clungunford, referred to in the well-known rhyme as being one of the four 'prettiest villages under the sun' – the others being Clun, Clunton, and Clunbury. Bucknell is small, but has a public school at Bedstone, north of the village on the up side. On the railway, there is the first of several level crossings with no gates; only traffic lights against road vehicles and a flashing white light to tell the driver if the traffic lights are working. Some other crossings have no gates or lights and some halts have unlit platforms, so the trains carry powerful spotlights for safety.

Knighton is an interesting town – situated in Wales with station standing in England. It is a centre for exploring Offa's Dyke Footpath, which stretches from the North to South Wales coasts. There is a Dyke Centre in the town, and visitors might care to join the speculation as to why King Offa of Mercia built the Dyke in the first place, over a thousand years ago.

Having crossed the border, the line soon begins to climb away from the Teme Valley through Knucklas (Cnwclas), and across the thirteen-arch castellated viaduct, some of the stone for which is said to have come from the medieval castle on the hill on the south side of the village. The train is now climbing at 1 in 60, and it becomes clear why the unusual two-coach DMUs on this line have to be among the most powerful in the country.

The 637-yard-long Llangynllo Tunnel brings us to the summit of the line at 980 feet above sea-level – the highest remaining on a standard-gauge railway in Wales. After the halt, we round a 90 degree curve, and the village of Llangynllo can be seen over a mile away on the valley floor.

We come to Llanbister Road and Dolau before reaching Pen-y-bont. Near here a railway was once planned to cross the Heart of Wales line on its way from England to Aberystwyth – its promoters would have been hard pressed to find a suitable route round the almost treeless slopes of Radnor Forest at 2,000 feet, which can be seen on the down side just before the short Pen-y-bont Tunnel is entered.

Llandrindod Wells is the county town of Powys, and is the main centre of population on the line between Church Stretton and Ammanford, despite having no more than 4,500 inhabitants. On the down platform is an inscription to mark the spot where, in 1952, Queen Elizabeth II first set foot in Wales after her accession to the throne, when she opened the Claerwen Reservoir in the Elan Valley. Llandrindod has wide, elegant Edwardian streets, a reminder of its past glory as one of Britain's leading spa towns, when the trains included through carriages from London and elsewhere, and up to 10,000 visitors arrived by rail each season. Llandrindod's revival as a resort seems to be gathering pace, which should boost rail traffic. A very special annual event is the week-long Victorian Festival, held in September.

Rail enthusiasts will have noticed that at Llandrindod the token exchange equipment is operated by the train-driver: all signal-boxes between Craven Arms and Pantyffynnon have been closed, and the Pantyffynnon signalman now supervises the driver's use of token instruments at each passing loop. The points giving entry to passing loops are locked automatically for the left-hand line as trains approach. Colour-light 'point indicators' can be seen – where there would normally be signals – to show that the points are correctly set. This system has drastically reduced the operating costs on the line, thereby helping to secure its future, and also making the operation of special trains outside normal 'opening hours' much cheaper.

At Builth Road, the Heart of Wales line passes over the route of the Mid Wales line from Moat Lane to Brecon (closed in 1962), which followed the course of the River Wye for much of its distance. Builth Wells is a pleasant market town about 1½ miles away to the left, and the Royal Welsh Agricultural Society's showground lies just outside the town.

Our train now climbs away from the Wye through the short Rhosferig and Cefn-y-bedd Tunnels to Cilmeri in the Irfon Valley: here can be seen, on the hill above the platform, the monument to Llywelyn the Last, Prince of Wales, who was reputedly killed here by the English in 1282.

After Garth, we reach Llangammarch Wells, another of the spas of Mid Wales, which, along with Llandrindod, Builth, and Llanwrtyd, was well publicised by the London & North Western Railway and its successor, the London Midland & Scottish Railway.

Llanwrtyd Wells itself has a passing loop and serves a village of about 500 people – reputedly the smallest community in the country to have been administered by an Urban District Council. Pony-trekking is a major activity here in the season, and the Cambrian woollen-mill is well worth a visit. Popular events include a beer festival and even a 'man against horse' race.

The scenery becomes more mountainous as the train climbs at 1 in 80 to Sugar Loaf Summit, some 820 feet above sea-level, where the tiny platforms that formerly served the signalmen and their families can be clearly seen. The station has been reopened on special occasions in recent years, and it may become a permanent request halt for country-lovers. Emerging from the 1,000-yard-long tunnel, we are on a ledge on the hillside, descending at 1 in 60, with a magnificent view to the south across the Vale of Tywi. Cynghordy Viaduct is an impressive eighteen-arch structure, built on a curve, and the halt is sometimes busier than might be expected; for, as with so many others on the line, its remoteness rules out a daily bus service.

Llandovery, like Builth Wells, is a typical Welsh market town, having Llandovery College, a small public school and the remains of a castle. The town, known in Welsh as Llanymddyfri, is the gateway to the Brecon Beacons National Park.

From Llandovery the railway follows the Tywi through Llanwrda and Llangadog, the latter having a creamery which is no longer rail-connected.

Until 1963, Llandeilo was the junction for Carmarthen, the branch swinging to the right just beyond the Tywi Bridge south of the station. This was a useful cut-off to West Wales, today's passengers having to make a detour via Llanelli. The brick-built signal-box is curiously out of character: it was opened in 1955 to replace three others in the vicinity. Note the elegant pedestrian suspension bridge over the river on the down side. Dynevor Castle is to be found on a hill to the west of the town.

Beyond Ffairfach, the line climbs quite steeply at 1 in 105, and on sharp curves which suggest its antiquity; it was an 1857 extension of the Llanelli Railway, which had opened in 1839 from Llanelli to Pontarddulais, and in 1841 was carried on to Duffryn (now Ammanford). The closed station of Derwydd Road is passed, and on the up side at Cilyrychen crossing can be seen the quarries which used to be connected to the mainline by a siding known as the 'Limestone branch'.

After Llandybie, we come to Ammanford. This was formerly known as Tirydail, to distinguish it from Ammanford Station on the Great Western Railway branch from Brynamman, which we join at Pantyffynnon. The Llandeilo–Pontarddulais section was actually owned by the GWR, but the LNWR exercised 'running powers' over it to reach Swansea.

Slag-heaps can now be seen on the up side, and on the same side at Tirydail crossing is the trackbed of the Mountain branch; this colliery line included rope-worked inclines as steep as 1 in 12. Pantyffynnon has a small but quite busy freight yard, despatching several coal trains each day to a variety of destinations. At the signal-box our driver hands over the single-line token for the last time: from now on we are controlled by the modern Port Talbot box, about 22 miles away by rail.

Although the scenery is now less striking, the route is still of great interest. Pontarddulais had a small marshalling yard, and was the junction for the LNWR mainline to Swansea Victoria, which was closed in 1964. All trains now bear right, through the short and narrow Hendy Tunnel to Llanelli. *En route*, at Hendy and Morlais Junctions, the Heart of Wales line forms a triangle with the Swansea District line, opened by the GWR in 1913 to allow its freight trains and Fishguard boat expresses to avoid the congestion and steep gradients in the vicinity of Swansea.

The Loughor (Llwchwr) Estuary is now on the down side of the line, and there is a good view of the most northerly part of the Gower Peninsula. As the line becomes double track once again we reach Llangennech and then Bynea on our way to Llandeilo Junction, where we join the main Swansea to West Wales route. On the up side is the large Trostre steelworks. Soon we reach Llanelli Station where our train reverses for the last stage of its journey to Swansea. Llanelli is a busy industrial town with a population of 28,000; it has a large shopping centre and a covered market, and forms a focal point for the valleys stretching away to the north.

The Shrewsbury to Swansea route is vital to the areas it serves. For some villages it is the only daily public transport service. Its links with north-west England, the West Midlands, and South Wales help reduce the isolation of rural Mid Wales. It also helps to sustain the local tourist trade, and is by far the shortest and cheapest rail line between south-west Wales and many parts of England.

But despite its importance and scenic beauty, the line has often been under threat of closure. However, in November 1981, a group of supporters decided that the decline had gone far enough, and formed the Heart of Wales Line Travellers' Assocation to try to preserve and develop the route. Membership now stands at 1,100 and includes many local councils and organisations.

Note
Due to storm damage to a bridge at Glanrhyd, a connecting bus service is temporarily replacing trains between Llandeilo and Llandovery. It is expected that through rail services will resume about the end of 1988.

NEWPORT–CARDIFF
by Adrian Fawcett

Leaving Newport, the imposing Civic Centre can be briefly seen to the right, before the train enters the ½-mile tunnel under Bryn Hyfryd upon which the oldest part of the town is built. There are in fact two parallel tunnels, most passenger trains taking the newer right-hand one. After the tunnel comes Gaer Junction, and then the freight-only line to Ebbw Vale climbs away steeply to the right. Once-extensive marshalling yards lie to the left, beyond which can be glimpsed the historic transporter bridge.

Once the Ebbw River is crossed Newport is soon left behind, and the four-tracked line curves to the right on to the Wentlooge Level, used principally for cattle-grazing. The next 5 miles are dead straight, and although the sea is just a mile away, coastal defences keep it from view. The village of Marshfield, location of a large Unigate dairy, is passed on the right, and farther on, urban development gradually approaches from the right as the outer suburbs of Cardiff are reached. A striking new viaduct passes overhead. This carries a new link road to Cardiff Docks, and the structure is of interest since its concrete sections are largely held together by glue. Almost immediately after comes Rumney river bridge, followed by a container yard on the left.

As the train slows on the approach to Cardiff Central Station, a disused canal can be glimpsed. It once carried coal from the Taff Valley to Cardiff Docks and before the railways came similar canals were to be found in many of the South Wales valleys.

The line from Queen Street crosses over us obliquely and descends to our left. This viaduct enables the suburban lines in Cardiff to operate without conflicting with the main lines, and use almost exclusively one island platform, Nos 6 and 7. There are two further island platforms, one pair being used for eastbound services and one pair for westbound services, as a general rule.

CARDIFF
by Paul Jeffries

Cardiff, capital city of Wales, is today a thriving commercial and administrative centre whose population exceeds 275,000. Its prosperity was founded upon the coal export trade which led to the development of extensive docks. The first railway to serve Cardiff was the Taff Vale in 1840; connection to the national network came in 1850 with the opening of the South Wales mainline. Today, rail plays a significant role in local transport; there are twenty passenger stations within the city boundaries, no fewer than seven of them newly opened in the 1980s.

The shopping centre is well served by rail, with Queen Street Station at its eastern and Central at its western ends. National chain stores are well represented, and the St David's Centre provides a modern indoor shopping mall, but there is still room for many smaller specialist shops in the city's fascinating arcades. Cardiff Castle dominates the city centre, its Norman keep contrasting with the Victorian opulence of its clock-tower and main apartments.

A little to the north, served by Cathays Station, stands the Civic Centre, where the modern styles of the Welsh Office and UWIST buildings blend happily with the classical architecture of the National Museum of Wales, Mid Glamorgan County Hall, University College, and the civic buildings. To the south, served by Bute Road, lie the docklands, where the new South Glamorgan County Hall symbolises the planned rejuvenation, while past glories are recalled in the Industrial and Maritime Museum.

The city's Anglican Cathedral, at Llandaff is, unusually, in a suburban location, ¾ mile from Fairwater Station. It stands alongside the River Taff, and riverside walks extend from the city centre all the way to Radyr. Cardiff is particularly well endowed with parkland; the Heath stations, for example, are close to Roath Park with its extensive boating-lake and Heath Park.

Sporting enthusiasts will need no introduction to the National Stadium, home of Welsh rugby, or to the Wales Empire Pool and Wales National Ice Rink, all close to Central Station. Ninian Park Station serves Cardiff City's soccer ground. Llanishen Leisure Centre, featuring indoor sports and a wave-making 'fun pool', stands ½ mile from Ty Glas Station.

Drama, opera, and ballet regularly feature at the New Theatre near Queen Street and the Sherman Theatre by Cathays Station, while concert-goers – classical and pop – have the St David's Hall in The Hayes, near Central Station. Truly, Cardiff is a city with something for everyone.

CARDIFF VALLEY LINES
by Paul Jeffries

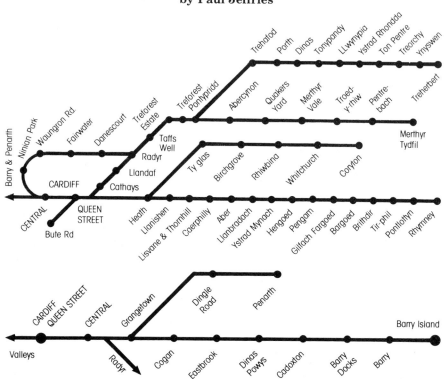

Cardiff Valley Lines comprises a self-contained network of routes radiating from Cardiff to serve the counties of South and Mid Glamorgan, extending to Penarth and Barry in the south, and to Treherbert, Merthyr Tydfil, Rhymney, and Coryton in the north – in total some 76 route miles, with sixty-one stations. A further 7 miles is to be added in 1988 with the reopening of the Aberdare branch. These lines represent the survivors of a veritable spider's web of competing routes laid down in the heyday of the South Wales coalfield by railway companies fighting for a share of the lucrative coal traffic. The oldest was the Taff Vale Railway, whose mainline from Bute Road to Merthyr, with a branch to Dinas, opened in 1840–41; this company later reached out to Aberdare in 1846, to Treherbert in 1856, and to Penarth in 1878. The Rhymney Railway, from a junction at Taffs Well, opened its line through to Rhymney in 1858, adding the direct line from Cardiff via Caerphilly in 1871. The Barry Railway built the line from Cogan Junction to Barry in 1888–89 and extended it to Barry Island in 1896. Finally came the Cardiff Railway, whose Heath Junction–Coryton line opened in 1909.

Strictly speaking, the Barry, Penarth, and Coryton lines do not serve the 'valleys' at all. From the shores of the Bristol Channel, these lines traverse the broad coastal plain, and the mountains are not encountered until beyond Radyr and Lisvane stations. The transformation in scenery north of these points is abrupt and remarkable, the trains then following the valley floors dominated by high ground on either side.

So much for history and geography: what is there for today's traveller to see? Working roughly from south to north, we may begin at Barry Island. Ever a popular resort with its safe, sandy beaches at Jackson's Bay and Whitmore Bay and its lively amusement park, the island – nowadays firmly connected to the mainland – is dominated by the Majestic Holiday Camp, which is open to day visitors as well as the resident holiday-maker. All these attractions are within a stone's throw of Barry Island Station. Travelling towards Cardiff, the train gives views across the Barry Docks, and at Cogan Station serves the adjacent Vale of Glamorgan Leisure Centre, before joining the line from Penarth.

In contrast to Barry, Penarth presents a rather sedate, Victorian splendour in its town centre, standing high above the cliffs of Penarth Head. Close by the station is the Turner House Art Gallery, where classical and modern styles both feature. A pleasant walk through Alexandra Park leads down to the Esplanade and the pier, still served in the summer months by Bristol Channel pleasure-steamers. The Penarth branch makes a steep descent to Cogan Junction, and there are views across the old Penarth Docks, now finding new life as a marina development takes shape, before the line sweeps alongside the Ely River to enter Cardiff, whose attractions have already been described.

Taking first the Taff Vale route northwards from Cardiff, perhaps the most dramatic scenery of the whole network is encountered beyond Radyr, where we run right alongside the River Taff and see on both sides the hills closing in, leaving only the narrow Nantgarw Gap through which railway, road, and river and formerly, canal, squeeze into Taffs Well. The east side is dominated by Castell Coch, William Burgess's romantic Victorian imitation of the Gothic style. The castle itself, unfortunately, is some 1½ miles and a steep climb from Taffs Well Station. As the valley broadens out again, reminders of King Coal are quickly evident. Throughout the valleys, though, nature and land reclamation schemes are slowly disguising the disfigurations of a century and more of indiscriminate spoil-tipping.

Treforest Station serves the campus of the Polytechnic of Wales, and soon we reach Pontypridd, where the grandiose station is a reminder of a bygone 'Golden Age'. The town is noteworthy for its excellent market held on Wednesdays and Saturdays, and the elegant early arched packhorse bridge over the Taff, dating from 1755. The nearby Pontypridd Historical and Cultural Centre gives a fascinating insight into local history and custom. In the pleasant Ynysangharad Park there is an outdoor swimming-pool, popular in summer, while first-class Rugby Union is played at Sardis Road, not far from the station.

Merthyr trains face a steep and long climb from Abercynon up to Merthyr Vale, scene of the Aberfan tragedy in 1966, before reaching their High Street terminus. Once Wales's largest town, today there are few reminders of those times when the iron industry dominated everything. Perhaps readers of Alexander Cordell's novels will think those days best forgotten, but Cyfarthfa Park and its Castle Museum, once the family seat of the Crawshays, is worth a visit. The opposite end of the social scale is represented by the terraced-cottage home of Dr Joseph Parry, the great Welsh composer of the nineteenth century, at Chapel Row. Certain trains are met at Merthyr Tydfil Station by a coach service giving onward connection through the Brecon Beacons National Park to Brecon itself.

Retracing our steps, Abercynon is to be the junction for the Aberdare service. This line closely follows the River Cynon, passing the Phurnacite plant at Abercwmboi whose fire-breathing chimneys form an eerie sight by night, to a terminus adjacent to the Aberdare swimming-pool with its spectacular 150-foot water-slide. From the centre of Aberdare there is access to the extensive Dare Valley Country Park, catering for all manner of outdoor pursuits. Walkers, for example, may enjoy the Dare-Amman

Ystrad Rhondda – one of the new stations in the Valleys, being served by a Barry Island–Treherbert train. (*Photo:* Tom Heavyside)

Trail, following a former railway trackbed from the park's Visitor Centre through to Cwmamman.

The Treherbert line has its junction at Pontypridd, whence it follows the valley of the Rhondda Fawr. Once synonymous with steam-coal, all its collieries are now closed, and the appearance of new light industry is only slowly imparting new life to a depressed area. Many once-proud chapels and workmen's halls are now derelict or neglected, although one exception is the Parc and Dare Hall at Treorchy – world famous for its male voice choir – which has been excellently restored. But outdoor activities dominate the Rhondda's attractions: the Glyncornel Centre at Llwynypia, for example, caters for environmental studies and sports such as archery, as well as offering Youth Hostel facilities, while from the line's rather bleak Treherbert terminus there is a minibus link onwards to Blaenrhondda and Blaen-y-cwm, whence hill and forest walks lead upwards toward the Rhigos Mountain.

The Rhymney line from Cardiff climbs slowly through the suburbs, throwing off its branch line to Coryton at Heath Junction, and serving both new housing developments and the Cefn-onn Country Park at Lisvane and Thornhill Station, before passing through a 1.1-mile-long tunnel – the only significant tunnel on the Valley Lines – to reach Caerphilly. Here stands the magnificent and enormous thirteenth-century castle, moated on three sides and, since the Civil War, boasting a 'leaning tower'. It ranks among the foremost surviving medieval fortresses of Europe.

Just under a mile east of the station is the site of the former railway workshops, where the Caerphilly Railway Society maintains an interesting collection of small steam locomotives; there are regular 'steam days' in the summer months. Once the convergence of five railway routes, only the Rhymney line now continues northwards from Caerphilly. If no less depressed than the Rhondda, the Rhymney Valley is perhaps greener and more scenic, and certainly narrower. At Hengoed, there still stands the fine stone-arch viaduct by which the old Pontypool–Neath line strode across the valley, while at Bargoed the Rhymney line itself bridges the river on its own lofty viaduct. The Stuart Crystal glass factory at nearby Aberbargoed welcomes visitors. Only a single-track continues on to Rhymney, northernmost outpost of the Valley Lines; although less than 4 miles, as the crow flies, from Merthyr Tydfil, Rhymney is the railhead station for Tredegar and a considerable area of the 'heads of the valleys'. Like Merthyr, Rhymney's roots lie in the early days of the iron industry, but here, too, little tangible evidence has survived.

A Valley Lines Day Ranger ticket, very reasonably priced at £3, offers the visitor a full day to explore this unique little network with its intensively worked services (Queen Street Station sees 300 trains each weekday) and its mixture of rural, industrial, and suburban scenery. Both South and Mid Glamorgan County Councils have contributed substantial capital investment in recent years, enabling 5 miles of line and ten new stations already to have been added in the 1980s; and, with further schemes being investigated, the future looks rosy for the Valley Lines.

Since 1987, most trains on the Valley Lines network have been operated by new Sprinter diesel units.

BRECON MOUNTAIN RAILWAY
by Paul Jeffries

Some 2½ miles north of Merthyr Tydfil stands the Pant terminus of the Brecon Mountain Railway Company, a remarkable narrow-gauge steam-operated railway opened in 1980 and largely following the trackbed of the former Brecon–Dowlais

Youngsters are shown how it works at Pant, on the Brecon Mountain Railway. (*Photo:* Tom Heavyside)

mainline which was closed in 1964. Pant Station, newly built by the company, is an exceptional construction neatly combining the functions of railway station, workshops, and restaurant in a single building architecturally following the Welsh Chapel style.

The train passes the remains of the Vaynor Quarries before panoramic views open up along the Taf Fechan Valley. Entering the Brecon Beacons National Park, the line currently finishes at Pontsticill Station, close to the dam wall of the Taf Fechan Reservoir. From here, there is a variety of country walks, including a 4½-mile circuit of the reservoir. The company has plans to extend further into the National Park as funds permit.

CARDIFF–WEST WALES
by Ken Davies and Tim Young

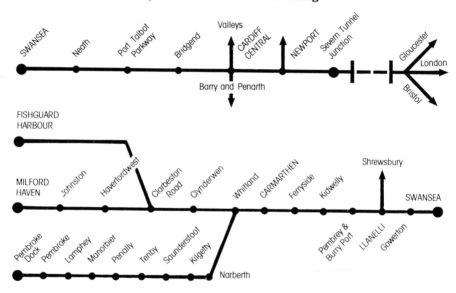

Immediately on leaving Cardiff Central Station and before crossing the River Taff, we see on the right the large Wales Empire swimming-pool, itself dwarfed by the soaring reinforced-concrete grandstands at Cardiff Arms Park, the venue for international Rugby football matches. The ground is so convenient to Cardiff Station that a large number of special trains are operated on each occasion when England, Scotland, Ireland, and France challenge the Welsh supremacy in what is, with choir-singing, the principal Welsh relaxation.

Canton diesel depot, including part of the former steam shed, lies to the left and, behind it, parallel with the mainline, runs the newly opened City line which created history by being the first significant passenger service to be introduced over a former freight-only line in Wales for very many years.

A few miles farther on, St Fagans Castle comes into view, standing on higher ground above some of the few thatched cottages we will see on our journey west. The castle is the central feature of the Welsh National Folk Museum; the station of that name disappeared over twenty years ago but there is an hourly bus service from Cardiff Central Station forecourt.

Derelict viaducts and trackbeds on both sides of the line just beyond St Fagans are all that is left of the former Barry Railway's avoiding line to Barry Docks, and exchange sidings. A nest of moth-balled sidings at Llantrisant are all that remain of this one-time busy junction for both passenger and coal trains. The station of this name was actually in the village of Pontyclun; Llantrisant itself, now the home of the Royal Mint, stands on the hilltop some distance away to the north.

In five places along our route the mountains come down to the sea, creating summits with long climbs on either side. Much of each slope is gradual but the maximum gradients are 1 in 106 up to Llanharan, 1 in 79 up to Stormy Sidings west of Bridgend, 1 in 88 up to Skewen some 2 miles beyond Neath, 1 in 50 from Swansea to Cockett Tunnel, and another 1 in 50 down to sea-level at Fishguard.

British Coal has moth-balled its opencast coal-treatment plant and nest of sidings on the left at Llanharan, hoping for planning permission for further surface workings, but public opinion has moved against the disturbance caused by this method of extracting coal.

Approaching Bridgend we see the site of a former Royal Ordnance factory, which had an extensive network of sidings serving virtually every building. This was converted into one of the first Industrial Estates and many factories continued to be rail-connected, mainly for boiler-house coal delivery, for another twenty years. While this rail connection was phased out, another came in to serve the Ford Motor Company's Bridgend engine plant. This joins the Vale of Glamorgan line about a mile from Bridgend Station and is a rare example of a new light-controlled level crossing, over the A48 trunk road.

The Vale of Glamorgan line diverges from the Cardiff–Barry Island line at Barry Station and follows the coastal plain, with some wide views of the Bristol Channel. This line comes in on the left just before Bridgend Station and is mainly used for merry-go-round coal trains to Aberthaw power-station but also is available as a diversionary route when the mainline via Llantrisant is unavailable. Leaving Bridgend, the line to Tondu climbs away on the right; the fan of colliery (and former passenger) branch lines beyond Tondu are either closed or lifted, except for the Maesteg Washery connection. There are proposals to reinstate a passenger service to Maesteg.

Half-way down the long incline from Stormy Down we see traces on the left of the closed Pyle Station and Porthcawl branch connections. At the foot of the incline a flyover bridge brings a connection from Tondu in on the left, with a corresponding flat connection on the right. By reversing at Tondu, trains can bypass most of the Bridgend–Port Talbot mainline so that there is an alternative route virtually all the way from Cardiff to Port Talbot.

Margam diesel depot and wagon repair shops are also on the left, followed by Margam Knuckle Yard and British Steel's Margam works, which extends almost to Port Talbot Station. Between Cardiff and Port Talbot we probably will have passed a bulk iron-ore train comprising twenty-eight wagons with a gross weight of 100 tonnes each, conveying the product from Port Talbot Docks to Llanwern steelworks, east of Newport.

To complete the industrial picture along this part of the journey, BP Chemicals have, on the left at Briton Ferry, a rail-connected plant, which is best seen after dark when the plant, and its associated towers, are brilliantly lighted in an intriguing pattern.

In direct contrast with the industry of the coastal belt to our left, the mountains come near to the sea from Pyle onwards, forming an impressive backdrop which is especially colourful in autumn.

The Swansea avoiding line leaves us on the left just after Briton Ferry (and joins the up line by a burrowing junction), then we pass on the same side a levelled site which once housed Neath locomotive shed and workshops. There were steel, tinplate, and copper works most of the way from Briton Ferry to Llanelli, both adjoining the mainline and the Swansea avoiding line but modern production methods combined with deindustrialisation have seen the end of these and of the slag-heaps made up of their waste products.

We pass Neath, home of the first known railway line in the world, with a glimpse of its Norman castle just beyond the station on the right, and, after crossing at right angles over the former Vale of Neath Railway, climb to Skewen. Beyond the village a short stretch of the Swansea avoiding line can be seen on our right after it emerges from a tunnel lying beneath us. As the line starts to descend to Landore, we pass under three stone arches with no obvious use; in fact they exist to revet the sides of the cutting – typical Brunel pragmatism.

Landore diesel depot, on our right, lies within the triangle formed by the mainline to West Wales and the Swansea East and West loops, Swansea Station being on a 'branch', but as all but a few seasonal trains stop here, it is in effect on the mainline.

Swansea, or Abertawe in Welsh, is known as the gateway to West Wales and the Gower Coast, and with a population of over 170,000 is the principal city in south-west Wales. It was created a city in 1969 by the Prince of Wales a few days after his investiture at Caernarfon Castle. Situated in Swansea Bay at the mouth of the River Tawe Swansea has long been a port. The area surrounding the South Dock has recently been redeveloped for leisure and housing, and incorporates an industrial and maritime museum. Close by in Oystermouth Road is Swansea's £4,000,000 leisure centre. Dylan Thomas was born in Swansea, and the city has become an important centre for the arts. In addition to the theatres, cinemas, museums, and art gallery, there is the annual Swansea Music Festival each October.

The city can also boast a good shopping centre, including the largest market in Wales, and offering a wide selection of local products. The local delicacy is laverbread, made from a species of seaweed which is first boiled to a black pulp, then fried with cockles and bacon.

The world's first passenger railway, closed in 1961, ran from Swansea to Oystermouth and Mumbles Pier, graduating from horse, through steam, to electric traction with a diesel shunter for good measure. Most of the route is now a public foot and bicycle path, as is the course of the lower reaches of the Central Wales line, from Swansea to Gowerton.

The Gower Peninsula, with its many miles of golden sands, is easily reached from Swansea. It was the first area in Britain to be designated an Area of Outstanding Natural Beauty and is a popular destination for day trips in South Wales.

From Swansea Station, our train climbs steeply to the summit at Cockett Tunnel, passing the closed Cockett Station, then drops equally sharply to Gowerton, a station sadly lacking in any facilities. Another closed station is still evident at Loughor with the ruins of a Roman fort called Leucarum overlooking the line from a hill. We cross the Burry Inlet, an arm of Carmarthen Bay, with views across the water to the north side of the Gower Peninsula. Leaving the open water, we see the western end of the Swansea avoiding line and Heart of Wales line coming in on our right. The avoiding line is mainly used by bulk oil trains and strip-steel coil trains from Port Talbot steelworks to Velindre and Trostre strip-mills, the latter being visible just beyond the junction. The two strip-mills spelt the death-knell of the multitude of small tinplating works, lying between the mainline and Llanelli town centre and which were served by a network of street railways, mostly worked by Peckett four-coupled saddle tanks resplendent in green livery.

Llanelli is the junction station for the Heart of Wales line, and has full passenger facilities. The town is still known colloquially as 'Sospan' from the ditty sung at International Rugby football matches 'Sospan fach yn berwi ar y tan' – 'Little saucepan boiling on the fire'. Llanelli is the largest town in Dyfed, and most of its centre is pedestrianised, making it popular with shoppers.

Leaving Llanelli, we run along the Burry Inlet again, with the line to Cynheidre Colliery – the stub of the Llanelli & Mynydd Mawr Railway – leaving on the right. At Pembrey and Burry Port the inlet leaves us to enclose the site of the former Carmarthen Bay power-station, the forecourt of which is used by wind-power generators. The first of these is H shaped, the second like a giant three-bladed aeroplane propeller.

The former Burry Port & Gwendraeth Valley Railway left from a station adjoining the present one, to dive under the mainline following the bed of an earlier canal on its way to Cwm Mawr, an exercise which restricted the loading gauge so that only locomotives with a limited cab and chimney height could be used. Latterly, steam locomotives of the 1600 Class were employed, followed by Class 03 diesels. The line has been cut back at Coedbach and now connects with the mainline at Kidwelly, although the height constraints still apply and some Class 08 locomotives have been cut down to suit and given names in the process. These can often be seen at Kidwelly or Llanelli. Pembrey's main claim to fame is that in 1928 the first seaplane to fly the Atlantic landed here, and a year later the first woman to fly across landed here, too.

By the time we reach Kidwelly, we are well into rural scenery and have left heavy industry behind. Kidwelly Castle is almost intact and forms an impressive backdrop to the town on the landward side of the line. At Ferryside we join the coast again, at the mouth of the River Towy, with a grandstand view of Llanstephan Castle across the water. The river follows the narrowing estuary, a haunt of wading birds, almost to Carmarthen. A few boat and seasonal trains avoid Carmarthen Station, using a triangle similar to the one at Swansea. All other trains reverse at the station, which has been a terminus since the closure of the cross-country lines to Llandeilo and Aberystwyth. Even the unique hog-back skew girder bridge which carried the railway across the Towy has now been removed 'to prevent flooding' – but the floods are still with us. Eight miles of the trackbed between Abergwili Junction and Llanpumpsaint have been acquired by the Gwili Railway Company, which operates steam tourist services for 2 miles beyond Bronwydd Arms. A bus connection runs from outside Carmarthen Station.

Carmarthen is a thriving market town, a short way uphill from the station, past what might be taken for a French château but is actually the County Council offices. The town's Welsh name, Caerfyrddin, means 'Fort of Myrddin', though only the gateway and towers of the castle remain today. Part of the Roman Fort of Moridunum has recently been excavated.

Leaving Carmarthen, the avoiding line rejoins us as we cross the River Towy by an unusual bascule bridge – now inoperable. The changing face of agriculture is typified by the opening of a timber railhead and two fertiliser railheads and the closure of a milk-processing plant. The Dairy Crest creamery straddling the River Gronw on the approaches to Whitland is still rail-connected, but such rail traffic as exists brings in milk for processing from Swindon.

Whitland Station, now completely rebuilt, is the junction for the Pembroke Dock branch, and also was the junction for the erstwhile Whitland & Cardigan Railway, which closed in 1962. Its grassy embankment may still be seen to the right after we cross the river. The next station, Clynderwen, is unusual in that it has staggered platforms. It is not staffed, but its original buildings remain. The initial route to Fishguard diverged here, but was replaced by the line via Clarbeston Road, which we now follow.

At Clarbeston Road, the Milford Haven branch sweeps off to the left, and our driver takes the token at the signal-box to permit us to travel on the single-track line to

Train for Swansea leaves Fishguard Harbour. (*Photo:* Tom Heavyside)

Fishguard. The scenery, until now mainly rolling open fields, becomes more woody. After passing through Spittal Tunnel we run alongside the Western Cleddau with rocky outcrops in places. The last stretch of line drops at 1 in 50 to sea-level, and after we have passed through the closed Fishguard and Goodwick Station Fishguard Bay spreads out before us with a cob leading out to a lighthouse in the middle of the bay, and the village of Fishguard farther to the right.

Fishguard Harbour Station has a single platform, and is primarily used by passengers connecting with the daily ferry service to Rosslare.

Fishguard was disguised as Llareggub for the film of Dylan Thomas's *Under Milk Wood.* Near by at Carreg Wastad the last invasion of Britain took place in 1797. Three French ships landed some 1,400 men who were repulsed by Lord Cawdor's army.

PEMBROKE DOCK AND MILFORD HAVEN BRANCHES
by Ken Davies and Tim Young

The Milford Haven branch leaves the Fishguard line at Clarbeston Road. From here, dedicated railway enthusiasts can take a 2-mile walk to Scolton Museum to see the oldest standard-gauge preserved locomotive with Great Western connections: named *Margaret,* it is a six-coupled saddle tank built in 1878, and acquired with the Gwendraeth Valleys Railway.

Trains run about every two hours between Swansea and Milford Haven, but note that there are no connections to or from Fishguard at Clarbeston Road. There is one High Speed Train each day to and from London Paddington.

About 5 miles from Clarbeston Road we come to Haverfordwest, the prosperous former county town of Pembroke, dominated by its castle which can be seen on the right on leaving the station. The remains of Haverfordwest Priory can also be seen after crossing the Western Cleddau River. The next station of Johnston was at one time the junction of the Milford Haven and Neyland lines. The latter used to be the mainline, since Neyland was the original terminus for steamer services to Ireland before they were diverted to Fishguard. The ferry to Pembroke Dock has also disappeared with the construction of the high-level road bridge over the River Cleddau. A branch to the left serves an oil refinery at Waterston, and a spur to the right serves Robeston refinery. Having collected the token at Johnston, we proceed on the single line dropping down to sea-level at Milford Haven whence there is a steep climb up to the town which is elevated above the haven, with commanding views from the promenade. Originally a fishing port, this large natural harbour commended itself to the multi-national oil companies who have set up four oil-discharge terminals. Some of the products go out by rail, but there are pipelines to the Midlands and Llandarcy, near Swansea. The harbour was once described by Nelson as 'the best in the world'.

Before crossing the bridge to travel on the line from Pembroke Dock, a general word about what used to be the County of Pembroke, or the southern part of it called 'Little England Beyond Wales'. The English influence is reflected in the place-names, very few of which have any feeling for the native language, but the Welsh are an obstinate lot and the current British Rail pocket timetables revive original names including the tongue-twisting Aberdaugleddau ('At the mouth of the two Cleddaus'), surely more of a meal than Milford Haven. The landscape is also very similar to that of south-west England.

Pembroke Dock must have been one of the first New Towns, built to house those who worked in the Royal Naval Dockyard until 'London knows best' shut it down half a century ago, a blow from which it has never recovered. The first Royal Yacht, the *Victoria and Albert* was built here, and until quite recently there was a street railway extension from the mainline right into the dockyard.

The first station along the line is Pembroke, serving the original town. It has a spectacular castle which was the birthplace of Henry VII. The castle has a large cavern underneath it. The line sets off diagonally to cross from the north to the south seaboard, passing through Lamphey with its bishop's palace. Even so, the railway still contrives to be a mile north of the village, and the castle at Manorbier, though it is well worth a walk to view as it is one of the finest in South Wales.

Just outside Manorbier Station the train stops briefly to allow the guard to operate the level-crossing gates, and so back to the coast at Penally where the station has been reopened by the efforts of a charming and determined Lady Councillor. Just beyond Penally, Caldey Island can be seen in the distance.

Another mile brings us to Tenby, the jewel in the crown; an almost unspoilt seaside resort set on high cliffs above two superb beaches with a picturesque harbour between them. On Caldey Island is a monastery which can be visited from Tenby during the summer and here can be purchased perfume made by the monks. Tenby Station has three platforms, and is the only passing place for trains on the branch line.

In high summer, cars are now excluded from the town's main streets, in stark contrast to Saundersfoot where the main car park is on the sea-front. Saundersfoot Station is a mile and a half along a pleasant country road from the resort. If the reader is energetic, he is advised to take the coastal path from Tenby, a veritable switchback which also winds its way round a series of coves. If he is not so brisk, he is advised to get a front seat in the DMU for the best view ahead as the line climbs and twists through woodland before reaching a plateau.

Saundersfoot has another claim to fame, in that it had a mineral railway with the unique gauge of 4 feet 4 inches, bringing coal from a colliery to the east of the town through a series of tunnels hewn out of the rock. The tunnels now form part of a footpath.

At Kilgetty we start to climb again to a summit well named Cold Blow as there is nothing to stop the wind. We then run down a steep incline to Narberth Station, passing an ornamental garden on our left filled with numerous varieties of rhododendrons, and going through the curving Narberth Tunnel.

And so back to the mainline at Whitland, but after leaving Narberth look out for the still-extant medieval pattern of strip-farming with evenly spaced farmhouses.

FURTHER INFORMATION

Rail Timetables

British Rail publish a passenger timetable for the whole of Great Britain, of nearly 1,500 pages, in May and October each year. It can be bought at staffed stations and at booksellers, and is usually available in public libraries.

Staffed stations and BR Travel Agents can also supply, free of charge, timetable booklets and leaflets for individual lines or groups of lines; and leaflets giving information on special offers – Railcards, taking bicycles by train, etc.

Bus Services

Deregulation of bus services was introduced under the 1986 Transport Act. As a result, information about bus services given in a guide-book of this kind may soon become out of date, and we cannot accept any responsibility for changes that may have occurred since we went to press in February 1988.

Bus information may be obtained from the Transport Co-ordinating Officer of the respective County Council. The following bus companies were known to be operating in Wales and the Marches at the time of going to press:

Chester City Transport, Station Road, Chester, CH1 3AD.

Corvedale Transport, 15 Tower Street, Ludlow, Shropshire, ST8 1QN.

Crosville Motor Services Ltd, Crane Wharf, PO Box 15, Chester, CH1 3SQ.

Davies Bros, Blossom Garage, Pencader, Dyfed.

Inter-Valley Link, Mill Road, Caerphilly, CF8 3FF.

Islwyn Borough Transport Ltd, Penmaen Road Depot, Pontllanfraith, Blackwood, Gwent, NP2 2DL.

Merthyr Tydfil Borough Transport, Transport Office, Nantygwenith Street, Merthyr Tydfil, Mid Glamorgan, CF48 1BW.

Midland Red (West) Ltd, Heron Lodge, London Road, Worcester, WR5 2EW.

National Welsh, 33 West Canal Wharf, Cardiff, CF5 1DB.

Newport Transport Ltd, 160 Corporation Road, Newport, Gwent, NPT 0WF.

Richards Bros, Moylgrove, Cardigan, Dyfed.

Silver Line Coaches, Merthyr Tydfil.

South Wales Transport Co. Ltd, 31 Russell Street, Swansea, SA1 4HD.

Taff-Ely Borough Transport, Glintaff, Pontypridd, Mid Glamorgan, CF37 4BG.

Yeomans Canyon Travel, Bus Station, Commercial Road, Hereford, HR1 2BL.

Private Railways

Timetables for the principal private railways are contained in the British Rail timetable; or can be obtained direct from the individual companies.

Bala Lake Railway, Llanuwchlyn, Gwynedd.

Fairbourne Railway, Beach Road, Fairbourne, Dolgellau, Gwynedd, LL38 2PZ.

Ffestiniog Railway, Harbour Station, Porthmadog, Gwynedd.

Llanberis Lake Railway, Llanberis, Gwynedd, LL55 4TY.

Snowdon Mountain Railway, General Manager, Llanberis, Gwynedd, LL55 4TY.

Talyllyn Railway, Wharf Station, Tywyn, Gwynedd, LL36 9EY.

Welsh Highland Railway, Gelerts Farm Works, Madoc Street West, Porthmadog, Gwynedd, LL49 9DY.

Welshpool & Llanfair Light Railway, Llanfair Station, Llanfair Caereinion, Powys, SY21 0SF.

WHAT IS THE RAILWAY DEVELOPMENT SOCIETY?

The Railway Development Society is a national, independent, voluntary body which campaigns for better rail services, for both passengers and freight, and greater use of rail transport.

It publishes books and papers, holds meetings and exhibitions, sometimes runs special trains, and generally endeavours to put the case for rail to politicians, civil servants, commerce, and industry; as well as feeding users' comments and suggestions to British Rail management and unions.

The RDS has fifteen branches, covering the whole of Great Britain. The Secretary of RDS Wales is Adrian Fawcett, Editor of this book; the Severnside, Midlands, and North-West branches cover neighbouring parts of England described in the book.

Membership is open to all who are in general agreement with the aims of the Society and subscriptions (spring 1988) are:

Standard Rate: **£7.50.**

Pensioners, students, unemployed: **£4.**

Families: **£7.50** plus **£1** for each member of household.

Write to the National Membership Secretary, Frank Hastilow, 49 Irnham Road, Four Oaks, Sutton Coldfield, West Midlands, B74 2TQ.

For other information about the Society and its branches, write to the General Secretary, Trevor Garrod, 15 Clapham Road, Lowestoft, Suffolk, NR32 1RQ.

Throughout Great Britain are also over seventy local rail-users' groups affiliated to the RDS. Groups in Wales include:

Glamorgan Rail-Users' Federation, 54 Heol Erwin, Cardiff, CF4 6QR.

Heart of Wales Line Travellers' Association: Secretary, Mrs Joan Rees, Glanrhosan, Cilycwm, Llandovery, Dyfed, SA20 0TG.

North Wales Railway Circle, Llyswen, 3 Min Menai, Eithenog, Bangor, Gwynedd.

Shrewsbury–Chester Rail-users' Association, David Lloyd, Sunnyside, Station Road, Whittington, Oswestry, Shropshire, SY11 4BQ.

Wrexham–Birkenhead Rail-users' Association, Mr C. Stephenson, 40 Castle Street, Caergwrle, Clwyd, LL12 9DS.

Cambrian Coast Line Action Group, Chairman: Richard Williams, 14 Llys Dedwyd, Marine Road, Barmouth, Gwynedd, Wales.

INDEX

ISBN 0–7117–0333–7
© 1988 Railway Development Society
Published and printed in Great Britain by Jarrold and Sons Ltd, Norwich. 1/88.